What Christ Said

What Christ Said

Revisiting the Countercultural Sayings of Christ Jesus

ISAAC PORTILLA

WIPF & STOCK · Eugene, Oregon

WHAT CHRIST SAID
Revisiting the Countercultural Sayings of Christ Jesus

Copyright © 2022 Isaac Portilla. All rights reserved. Except for brief quotations in critical publications or reviews, no part of this book may be reproduced in any manner without prior written permission from the publisher. Write: Permissions, Wipf and Stock Publishers, 199 W. 8th Ave., Suite 3, Eugene, OR 97401.

Wipf & Stock
An Imprint of Wipf and Stock Publishers
199 W. 8th Ave., Suite 3
Eugene, OR 97401

www.wipfandstock.com

PAPERBACK ISBN: 978-1-5326-9495-0
HARDCOVER ISBN: 978-1-5326-9496-7
EBOOK ISBN: 978-1-5326-9497-4

VERSION NUMBER 022322

All Scripture quotations, unless otherwise indicated, are taken from the Holy Bible, New International Version®, NIV®. Copyright ©1973, 1978, 1984, 2011 by Biblica, Inc.® Used by permission of Zondervan. All rights reserved worldwide. www.zondervan.com The "NIV" and "New International Version" are trademarks registered in the United States Patent and Trademark Office by Biblica, Inc.®

Scripture quotations marked (ESV) are from the ESV® Bible (The Holy Bible, English Standard Version®), copyright © 2001 by Crossway, a publishing ministry of Good News Publishers. Used by permission. All rights reserved.

Scripture marked (NKJV) taken from the New King James Version®. Copyright © 1982 by Thomas Nelson. Used by permission. All rights reserved.

Contents

Acknowledgements | ix

CHAPTER 1
As I Have Loved You: The One Commandment | 1
   1. Love | 1
   2. Difficulty | 1
   3. Denial | 3
   4. The Word | 4
   5. Seeing God | 6
   6. The Way | 7
   7. The New Life | 8
      Truth | 10

CHAPTER 2
Why Do You Call Me Good? On Goodness and Perfection | 11
   1. The Aim | 11
   2. On Goodness | 12
   3. Who Is Good? | 13
   4. Opposite Culture | 16
   5. Toward Perfection | 17
   6. The Nature of Perfection | 19
   7. Living in the Light of Truth | 21
      Truth | 24

CHAPTER 3
Destroy This Temple: The Unbreakable Real Church | 25
   1. Who Understands? | 25
   2. Authority Is Christ's Body | 26
   3. The Bodily Temple | 28

    4. The Church of the Called | 30
    5. The Temple Church | 32
    6. The Institutional Church | 34
    7. The Unknown (Real) Church | 36
    Truth | 38

CHAPTER 4
Let the Dead Bury Their Own Dead: On Freedom from Family Constructs | 39
    1. The Call Is to Go Straight | 39
    2. Negotiation | 40
    3. Worry and Spiritual Family | 42
    4. Rejection of Inheritance | 44
    5. Universal Family | 47
    6. Beyond Childhood and Parenthood | 49
    7. No Home but God | 50
    Truth | 52

CHAPTER 5
Will Set You Free: Truth Explorations and Openings of Being | 53
    1. The Proof of Truth | 53
    2. Disciples and Freedom | 54
    3. The Threefold Teaching of Freedom | 56
    4. Truth and Freedom: The Test of Being | 58
    5. Sin and Truth | 60
    6. Preaching and Freedom | 62
    7. The Logos | 64
    Truth | 66

CHAPTER 6
God Is Spirit: The Experiential Fact of God | 68
    1. Spirit—the Real God | 68
    2. The Fact of God | 69
    3. The New Worship according to Christ | 71
    4. What God Is | 73
    5. Words and Divine Cognition | 74
    6. The Fact of God Remains in a Heartbreaking World | 77
    7. Reason, Science, and God | 79
    Truth | 80

CHAPTER 7
They Will Inherit the Earth: On Forgiveness and Meekness | 81
  1. The Blessed | 81
  2. Lightness of Being | 82
  3. The Two Doors of Forgiveness | 83
  4. Forgiveness and Gratitude | 85
  5. Earth—Home of Divine Descent | 87
  6. Entering Jerusalem | 89
  7. The Meek Can Be Taught by God | 90
     Truth | 92

CHAPTER 8
Take What Is Yours and Go Your Way: On Fairness and Justice | 94
  1. Abundance in Heart | 94
  2. The Fairness of the Just | 95
  3. Finding Fairness in Asking | 96
  4. Justice and Love | 98
  5. Christ—the Judged Who Is to Judge | 100
  6. On (False Testimony by) Being Judgmental | 102
  7. The Last Ones | 103
     Truth | 105

CHAPTER 9
How Can You Say, "Show Us the Father?" On God Realization | 106
  1. Philip's Asking | 106
  2. Those Who See God Are Blessed | 107
  3. The Absolute | 109
  4. God Realization and the World | 111
  5. The Glory of the Transfiguration | 114
  6. "I AM" | 116
  7. Knowing God Fully | 117
     Truth | 120

CHAPTER 10
I Will Not Leave You as Orphans: The Immanent Truth of Christ | 121
  1. The Christ Remained | 121
  2. A Culture of Becoming | 122
  3. The Immanent Christ | 124
  4. The Coming of the "Son of Man" | 126
  5. Back to the Father—the Mechanics of Exchange | 128

6. The Immanent Life in Matter | 130
7. Fruit of Living Fire | 132
   Truth | 134

Bibliography | 135

Acknowledgements

I WOULD LIKE TO show my gratitude to Professor Stanley Hauerwas (Duke University) for receiving me at his office for a series of meetings during the cold days of January 2018, and for his encouragement and advice regarding the publication of this book. It was during this research visit at Durham that I started working on chapter 1 (the only one I had drafted at the time).

I am grateful to Professor Mario Ignacio Aguilar (Director of the Centre for the Study of Religion and Politics, University of St Andrews) for his advice on the positioning of this book and his invitation to present it at the Scholars at the Peripheries Research Group, where it obtained a wonderful response.

Warm thanks to those who, with their feedback, helped me to shape a better version of this book: Dr. Daniel Spencer (University of St Andrews), for his insightful comments on chapter 2 and our follow-up conversation; Professor N. T. Wright (University of St Andrews, Senior Research Fellow at Oxford), for his valuable response to my inquiry on chapter 10; Juan Yusta, for his availability and help in the final revision, and for coordinating sessions and retreats where we have explored some of the themes presented in the book (specifically forgiveness, chapter 7).

Very specially, I thank Dr. Ralitza Nikolaeva (University of St Andrews), who read the entire manuscript and gave me excellent advice; also for her companionship and support in this life journey, and her encouragement to write on Christian topics.

I am grateful to Wipf and Stock Publishers for welcoming this project, and also for their trust and flexibility throughout the process.

CHAPTER 1

As I Have Loved You
The One Commandment

1. Love

Jesus said, "Love each other *as* I have loved you" (John 15:12, emphasis added). He did *not* say, "Love each other as you like," nor "Love each other as you can." No. He said, "Love each other *as* I have loved you."

Hence: for much that we fail to see it, for much that we are afraid to say it, we can love like Christ. We can love like Christ not because we want to, out of some grandiose desire of ours—to be like the Son of God—but because he said so; he said we shall love like him. Thus, we will not be proud when we assert this possibility, but faithful—to him. By loving in such a way, we will be contributing to the emergence of a renewed Earth; an Earth crafted by those who are coherent with the teachings of Christ, by those who serve as conductors of the Spirit's descent. To love as Christ is not just the way to be truthful to the words of Christ, it is Truth enabled. Such is the main sign of Christ carriers—of those who take the responsibility to be the Light in this world, of those who facilitate the transformation of the Earth.

2. Difficulty

Jesus said, "Love each other *as* I have loved you."

What Christ Said

The most striking implication of this statement is not the act of love—that is, to love one another—but the qualification of such love: that it shall be a Christ-like Love. Without this qualification of love, the one Christian commandment would be incomplete, thus ineffective. As for loving each other, Christ is not needed: Would we deny the existence of relational or fraternal love in the times before Christ, or in those who do not follow the Way of Christ? No, we cannot deny such love, neither in the times before the Light[1] came to stay nor in those who have not committed to the Way of endurance in the Light of being. Anyone who has traveled the world or established friendships beyond their own Christian community knows it: relational and fraternal love were not brought by Christ; Christ-like Love was brought by Christ.

Yet, some Christians forget the last part of the one commandment—as if the statement "*as* I have loved you" no longer existed. Such forgetfulness results in the mistaken divinization of affectionate love, because the "commandment," as they remember it, is to love each other. And so, certainly feeling affection for one another, they say among themselves: "We do love each other as Christ commanded us, don't we?" But they forget: you do not need to follow the Way of Christ to love kindly, passionately, compassionately, or in a brotherly, motherly, or fatherly way, because these types of love and affection are not the Gift of Christ. Hence, erroneously assuming Love is a Christian given—presumed "to be there" if you are a Christian—some Christians pay attention to just doing "the right thing," not giving enough consideration to the way they should love—as Christ did.

Of course, the commandment of Christ to love like him is much more difficult to contemplate than the accumulation of deeds sufficient to feel that one is "good enough" to be counted as the chosen sheep. But to love *as* Christ is *not* a Christian given. It cannot be bought by deeds, although it may be demonstrated in deeds; it cannot be thought of as affection, although it may be accompanied by affection. The command of Christ to love like him is difficult. It is difficult because it is inconvenient. It is inconvenient because it demands the questioning of our self and the transformation of our being. Even so, we should not allow the editing of Christ's words in our minds and our hearts. We should not allow the exile from our consciousness of the last part of the one Christian commandment just because it is inconvenient for us. We cannot say that to love one another is

---

1. Christ is the Light. See John 1:4; 3:19; 9:5; 8:12; 12:46.

the Christian commandment. Only the commandment to love *as* Christ is faithful to the words of Christ.

3. Denial

Jesus said, "Love each other *as* I have loved you."

Without this qualification of love, Christ is denied. That is, if we reject the possibility to love as Christ, we are denying the Christ in us—we decide to not-know the Light of being, and to not-be his living witnesses in the world. Moreover, by denying the Christ in us, we are refusing to embody the Way of Christ: we are battling his call (to follow him), his teaching (to be the Light of the world), and his prayer—that the love with which the Father loved him may be in us, and that he (the Light through and of which things are made) may be in us.[2] Even more, we are rejecting the fruit of his Sacrifice—the Atonement of our being for its participation in the Light of sentient creation, which is Christ himself, as Logos and Being.

Christ-like Love is dependent on Divine Light expressed in the context of human relationships. This Light is difficult to bear because it challenges our conceptions of "self" and "other" by calling us to perfection in Spirit, both as individuals and as a community. For this reason, many are those who misallocate Christian Love from the domain of divinized relationships to the context of superficial interactions, thus making it dependent *not* on Divine Light but on kindness. In these environments, Christ is imagined as a "sinless" Good Shepherd in whom the higher complexity of his mighty character—as Light, Life, and Truth—is absent. Accordingly, contemporary Christians emphasize kindness instead of Truth; politeness instead of Love. But Truth and *not* kindness, and Love and *not* politeness, is what Christ taught. Indeed, Christ was less kind than most well-minded Christians want to be and possibly are: Christ used the whip and turned over the tables of the money changers at the temple;[3] Christ did not wait for his called ones to bury their relatives;[4] Christ rejected brotherhood based on blood in front of his brothers and his mother;[5] Christ publicly called the religious leaders of his time "hypocrites!" and "brood of vipers!";[6] and Christ told the

---

2. John 17:26.
3. Matt 21:12; Mark 11:15; Luke 19:45; John 2:15.
4. Matt 8:22; Luke 9:59–60.
5. Matt 12:46–50; Mark 3:31–35; Luke 8:19–21.
6. Matt 23:13–33.

fruitless fig tree to wither away.[7] His power was not in his kindness but in the Father's will and the Spirit. Christ demanded truthfulness, forgiveness, commitment, insight, wisdom, and, above all, Love of divine standards—standards set by him, supported by conditions set by him through his Office and Sacrifice. Without the qualification of Love to be *as* Christ's—the standards set by the Son of God—Christ is denied as a matter of course.

On the other hand, by taking the responsibility of such Love, we will be demonstrating that we take him seriously. To take Christ seriously means, first, to sincerely try to understand him—to pay attention to his teaching and not to edit his words—then, to act consequently. If we do not acknowledge that Christ's commandment implies to love like him, we will be one step from mocking him. One day we will call him "Lord!" and he will say to us, "I do not know you."[8] Roman soldiers made a parody of Christ just by not understanding Christ, by misinterpreting Christ. They thought he was a fake, a self-proclaimed king. They mocked him; they beat him; they sealed their parody with a crown of thorns (a metaphor for their own imprisoned minds and so also for the world's mind) and spat on their Salvation. If we allow the editing of Christ's words in our hearts and souls, we will be one step from making a parody of him, one step from mocking him, as the soldiers—enactors of Roman rule—did. If we do not remember that the one Christian commandment implies a Christ-like Love, we will soon say: "We do love each other as we like, and possibly can, and that is sufficient for us." And for us it may be, but not for Christ, to whose sight and Being we may have become unrecognizable.

4. The Word

Jesus said, "Love each other *as* I have loved you."

Such a powerful and single commandment gives the Christian a place to focus and a standard to live by. Through the contemplation of Christ's commandment, our personal being is affirmed in Christ's Being, as we cannot love as Christ unless we are established in Christ. The observance of the one commandment is indicative of one's faith in the Christian belief that the Logos is the Word, and that the Word is the Light of being—the Light through and of which a person is made in a Christ-like manner. Thus, the commandment of Christ is of crucial importance not only because it is of

---

7. Matt 21:19–21; Mark 11:13–14.
8. This idea follows Matt 7:21–23 and Luke 13:27; however, it is not a direct quotation.

Christ, but also because it depends on Christ himself as the foundation of Life.

But, to have a single commandment may be perceived as a weakness to some, because it can be argued that if this passage of Scripture were not truthful to the original Word of Christ,[9] it would mean that Christianity would be left without commandment and that Christians would not have a distinctive standard by which they are to live. However, it would be quite an error to think that imprecise scriptural heritage may be giving us an unsecured one commandment, because to love like Christ is neither imposition, order, nor law, but the foundation and outcome of the Christian existence. That is, if Christian existence depends upon such a condition—to love like Christ—it is not as an adherence to an imposed law but as the very foundation and outcome of what means to *be* Christian, because the whole *atmosphere* of a Christian life is Love, by abiding in Christ. And so, Christ's commandment is *not* a rule or a law (as if it had been given in the same fashion as the stone tablets to Moses) but instead the compassionate way the Son of God gave us the North Star of our journey, so as not to get lost. Thus, the experience of living in Christ was worded, but it was *as if* Jesus were saying to his beloved ones: "No words would be needed and no commandment would be necessary for those who have understood with their being that I AM; but as you want one commandment, I will give you this one, that you shall love each other as I have loved you, so that you may see each other as I see you, so that you may behold the entire sentient creation in the Glory of the Light that I AM and in the magnificence of its genesis."[10]

Our acceptance of the Word of Christ is thus based not on blind belief but on our experience as carriers of Christ. As a result, we can assert that we shall love like Christ not only because Christ said we should but because Christ-like Love is the Christian experiential heritage. And because the Gift of Christ can be summed up in such manner, we shall be able to say the following: "Even if it were proven that Christ never uttered the one commandment, we know that such is the unuttered truth of his Gift to us; therefore, to love *as* Christ still remains our one commandment and North Star."

---

9. According to most scholars, Jesus' main language of communication would have been an ancient Galilean dialect of Aramaic; the dialect is believed to have been lost. It is likely that Jesus spoke other languages as well, including Hebrew and Koine Greek. See, for example, Fassberg, "Which Semitic Language."

10. My words, not Jesus Christ's.

5. Seeing God

Jesus said, "Love each other *as* I have loved you."

Those who accept that a Christian shall love *as* Christ must consequently ask: What does it mean to love like Christ? The answer, however, should focus not on the all-encompassing, nonjudgmental, forgiving, and sacrificial characteristics of Christian Love but, more fundamentally, on its very root and definition, because all these characteristics cannot be claimed as unique to Christianity if removed from the type of Love they sprout out of. To focus on the root of Christian Love means to focus on its cause: perception. That is, in the same way that all types of relational love depend on a certain type of perception—a certain way of acknowledging another person—Christ-like Love must depend on Christ-like perception. And so, the next question we need to answer is: What is Christ-like perception?

The answer is given in the Scriptures: "Blessed," said Christ, "are the pure in heart, for they will see God" (Matt 5:8). And God, the New Testament says, is Spirit, Light, and Love.[11] Thus, Christ-like perception means to see God. And to see God means to perceive the coessential Trinity—Spirit, Light, and Love—to abide in the Glory of an illuminated Divine Existence. Such a beautifully simple and scripturally supported definition of God is to be reclaimed once and again in the face of forgetfulness: Spirit, Light, and Love are, as they are, the Living God—the God that is a Living Reality for those who have "eyes" to see, for those called to love *as* Christ did. By reasoning in this manner, we shall now ask ourselves: How did Christ perceive his beloved disciples so that we may perceive our spiritual companions in like manner?

Christ saw God in everything and everyone, as must we. If we are to be enablers of a Love such as Christ's to flood this Earth existence, there is no other way to do it—we must come to see all living forms, the unmoving matter, the clear space, and so all there is with the same spiritual consciousness that Christ demonstrated. But especially, we must come to see the "other"—the human being before our eyes—in a Christ-like manner. Such divine acknowledgment of the "other" is most important, because Christ's commandment to love was referring to the human other, with a purpose: to show the way God's Love acts in creation—through *relationship*. Thus, by making the commandment not just "Love as I love" but "Love each other

---

11. John 4:24; 1 John 1:5; 1 John 4:16.

as I have loved you," every Christian became a recipient and enabler of a nascent Divine Existence.

6. The Way

Jesus said, "Love each other *as* I have loved you."

Once we accept that the one Christian commandment is not just to love but to love *as* Christ, and that such Love can only happen if we perceive the "other" as Christ did—by seeing God (i.e., Spirit, Light, and Love) in those our being can acknowledge in such manner—one subsequent question we need to answer is this: How can we come to see and abide in God? (We cannot hope our awareness will acquire Christ-like characteristics out of our good intentions but instead through a process of spiritual transformation brought about by Grace and divine signs.) Jesus' life shows us the path, since the mystical events of his lifetime were not experiences for himself but divine undertakings which opened a New Way for us to follow.

Jesus starts his ministry after a Divine Force descends on him, upon his Baptism in the river Jordan. Subsequently, he empowers his disciples with this Force, and his disciples empower others likewise.[12] Thus, our first reference is that of an empowerment, and we must follow it: we must receive the Divine Force through which Love acts in creation so that it may remain as a living, operating principle in our being.[13] And so, to know that "God is Love" (the Third Aspect[14] of the Trinity), we must be empowered by the Divine Force responsible for the dynamics of creation, a Force which opens our being to the *discovery* of its spiritual evolution.

Moreover, Christ conveyed to us that we are destined to be Light: "You are the light of the world" (Matt 5:14); "Believe in the light while you have the light, so that you may become children of light" (John 12:36). He further affirmed that our bodies would shine with splendor if we would just

---

12. John 3:22–26; 4:1–2.

13. Symeon the New Theologian referred to this Divine Force—to its experience—as a "spine-chilling mystery." He states: "What is this spine-chilling mystery that is being accomplished in me?" (Hymn 1, verse 1); "He Who is united with us, oh spine-chilling mystery! And thus it truly becomes a marriage, unutterable and divine" (Hymn 15, verses 174–75) (Symeon the New Theologian, *Hymns*). See also Hymn 21 regarding the ups and downs of the Spirit. This is an example of how the Spirit, as Force, is experienced in the Christian tradition.

14. "Aspect" of the Trinity means *hypostasis* (Greek).

remove the darkness preventing the Light within us from shining forth;[15] and he demonstrated this possibility to three of the apostles in the event of the Transfiguration, when his body became out-and-out Light and his face shone like the sun. Thus, to realize that God is Light (the Second Aspect of the Trinity) we must *recover* the Christ nature inherent in our being; we must seek the means to remove the psycho-physical darkness that prevents the Christ in us from being the luminous reality of our awareness and being.

Furthermore, Christ said that God must be worshiped "*in* the Spirit and *in* truth" (John 4:23–24, emphasis added). To realize that God is Spirit—the Truth[16] of our existence (the First Aspect of the Trinity)—we must seek to perceive the Source of our very being, the Absolute Reality in which all we see assuredly rests. "I am in the Father and the Father is in me" (John 14:11), said Christ. To gain such perception, we must allow our being to *return* to its existential home; we must fall in our faces and seek the transcendental embrace of our all-forgiving Father as exhausted and repentant prodigal sons.

Lastly, we shall ask for the blessing of the Regenerative Fire—a mystery of the Logos we cannot comprehend—and engage in the New Life with unlimited unknown possibilities. As Christ said, "the Holy Spirit . . . will teach you all things" (John 14:26). That is: things that Christ Jesus did not teach we shall learn. Moreover, Christ said, "whoever believes in me will do the works I have been doing, and they will do *even greater things* than these, because I am going to the Father" (John 14:12, emphasis added). Hence, we are meant to follow Christ's example through witnessing his Glory in our acts, not ignoring our failures ("failures" are not to be confounded with the difficulties of the Mystical Cross we must bear with gladness). In conclusion, we are to gain Christ-like perception and to *explore* the potentialities given to us by the Spirit, welcoming the challenges they may bring.

7. The New Life

Jesus said, "Love each other *as* I have loved you."

---

15. Luke 11:36.

16. In this work, God, the Father, the Absolute is the Truth; the Son—as Logos—is "the truth" (John 14:6); further, Christ's teaching leads to the truth (which is not an opinion-based truth), as explored in chapter 5. This capitalization will be used throughout the book.

This statement is Christ's differentiating commandment—the truly unique Christian commandment which distinguishes Christianity from any other spiritual path or tradition. It is true that Jesus paraphrased two commandments of the old law—to love God and to love your neighbor as yourself—thus confirming their importance.[17] But he did so when challenged by a scribe and so as a demonstration of his knowledge and all-embracing message, not as a teaching of his own. These two commandments belonged to the old law, but they ought to be reinterpreted through the law of Christ, which is acausal Grace—that is, Grace not based on religious righteousness, rules, and deeds but on Christ's Being. This is the reason Christ concluded this episode by saying to the scribe: "You are not far from the kingdom of God" (Mark 12:34).[18] As if saying that one is in the right direction when following these commandments, but still not abiding in the Living Light.[19]

Therefore, the former commandments were those of the uninitiated in the Way of Christ. But to love like Christ was the new commandment given to the beloved ones of Christ Jesus when alone, free from the public eye. The new commandment indicated the way they would be recognized and give living testimony of Christ—by their Christ-like Love manifested in the mutual contemplation of one another. And so, we must remember that the old law does not make a Christian to *be* Christian. For a Christian to love God means to have the aspiration to love like Christ, as there is no other way to guarantee that our love for God is true and complete and that it is corresponded by God's Love for us. Likewise, to love your neighbor means to love the "other" as Christ did, as Christians do not love themselves, but rather deny themselves to find their true self—the inherent Christ nature concealed within their false perception of self—so as to live and love from such a viewpoint (or else we will end up holding the odd notion that Christ loved others as he loved "himself").

---

17. Mark 12:30–31.

18. In the episode with the wealthy young man, Jesus also paraphrases "love your neighbor as yourself" to further say that this and other commandments are not enough to be perfect—one must follow him to be perfect (Matt 19:16–30). See chapter 2.

19. The two commandments of the old law—to love God and to love your neighbor as yourself—are often brought forth within interreligious/interfaith dialogue as a means to find common ground—a shared orientation—among faith traditions. However, acknowledging common values should not preclude exploring different contributions. Thus, interreligious/interfaith dialogue can be an opportunity for the Christian to reflect on the contribution of Christ-like Love to humanity and a call to embody such Love more consciously.

But still, Christians are constantly trapped in arguments around behavior—that is, around what a Christian should or should not do. Some Christians do not seem to rely on the power of the Living Christ—the Christ operating as a living principle in our being and awareness—and seek for fixed rules of conduct to determine their behavior and their judgment of others. But the strength and beauty of the Christian Way comes precisely through its undefined characterization when coming to human behavior. That is, instead of giving fixed rules of conduct ("When this happens, do so and so"; "Such is right, such is wrong"), the Christian Way provides divine insight through which behavior is to be explored by the act of living. Christ constantly challenged assumed-to-be-fixed rules of conduct by a living exploration of divine principles—principles that can only be understood when truly lived: the strict and rather passive observance of the Sabbath was challenged by compassionate works of healing in adherence with the Father's will; the stoning of the adulterous woman was confronted by increasing the awareness of the multitude's own sins.[20] Once and again, the Gospels portray the failure of fixed rules of conduct to represent divine principles. Christ demonstrates a different type of perception and understanding of reality which constantly surprises, because it comes as flexible behavior consistent with God's Love, not with humans' fears and dogmatic fixations.

Truth

Christ's Love is greater than mere human affection and the friendly apprehension of another person—it is Divine Love manifested in sentient creation; it is the power of the Logos recognizing our being as his own beloved creation. Overwhelming and humbling. Truthful and complete. Such is the Love that *lives in us* through Christ.

Jesus said, "Love each other *as* I have loved you." And it was his only commandment for all.

---

20. A Christian should be critical of these same tendencies when displayed in a Christian context. For example, to say, "Do not ever work on Sunday, because it is holy," would represent an attitude that reenacts the very behavior that Christ challenged.

CHAPTER 2

Why Do You Call Me Good?
On Goodness and Perfection

1. The Aim

JESUS SAID, "WHY DO you call me good? . . . No one is good—except God alone" (Mark 10:18).[1] Jesus said further, "Be perfect, therefore, as your heavenly Father is perfect" (Matt 5:48).[2] A radical conclusion follows: no person is "good," but we ought to be "perfect." Thus: perfection, not goodness, is the aim of Christian life.

Since Christ said we ought to be perfect, we are called to pursue perfection. But in realizing perfection, we shall not call ourselves "good"—we are not to think that we are a "good person"; we are not to assert that we are a "good Christian"; for Jesus himself rejected being called "good." Thus, we must work to attain perfection, knowing that we will not acquire the capacity of judging whether we are good, or whether any other person is good. That is, we shall follow the path of perfection living in ignorance of what it means to be good—*living in ignorance of judgment*. Hence, we are to let go

---

1. See also Luke 18:19 and Matt 19:17.

2. "Be perfect" tentatively denotes the completion of an aim through a process. See the Greek *teleios*, "*brought to completion*" or "*without shortcoming* in respect to a certain standard, Mt. 5:48" (Mounce, *Interlinear New Testament*, 1177). Such is the position of this inquiry: perfection is the Christian aim, while the Christian path is the process to reach perfection and, furthermore, encompasses any process that amplifies perfection. (Jesus called us to perfection in the Sermon on the Mount.)

of the burden of judging the goodness of others and to accept the freedom of not having to label ourselves as "good," not accepting such labeling from others either. In sum: Christians are to live in ignorance of their goodness, and all goodness expressed in a path of perfection will never suffice to assert that we are good; we are not to call ourselves "good" nor to accept anyone's opinion regarding our goodness as true. The Christian aim is not to be good but to be perfect. Thus, we shall pursue perfection.

2. On Goodness

Jesus said, "Why do you call me good? . . . No one is good—except God alone." Jesus said further, "Be perfect, therefore, as your heavenly Father is perfect."

But we know goodness, we may say—it is a feeling of calmness in God; it is the peace we experience in the presence of those who live a life dedicated to God, or when we live such a life ourselves. How is it, then, that we are not to judge either ourselves or others as "good"—never? Even Jesus—can we not say with certainty that Jesus was good?[3] Yet, the teaching of Christ is clear: if you say, "Jesus is good," then Jesus replies, "Why do you call me good? . . . No one is good—except God alone." That is, even if we acknowledge goodness as a major feature of a Christian's life, no amount of goodness qualifies a person to be called "good."[4] We may find peace in a life dedicated to God, but we shall enjoy such peace without the need to be content in our goodness.

Thus, in order to follow Christ, we must sacrifice our ideals—those of being a good person, a good Christian, a good community—so as to uphold Christ's call—to become perfect. Because being a good person, a good Christian, and a good community are ideals relying on a type of judgment we are not qualified to make, while being perfect—through communion with the Spirit and Truth—is an aim we are qualified to attain. Indeed, perfection is the aim of Christian existence, according to Christ; an aim that was given openly—"Be perfect, therefore, as your heavenly Father is

---

3. Jesus called himself the "good shepherd" (John 10:11–16), yet "good" here is in relation to his function and Office: "The good shepherd lays down his life for the sheep" (John 10:11). Such goodness, from the Greek *kalos*, seems to have a different and more aesthetic connotation than *agathos*, as used in Mark 10:18 and Luke 18:19.

4. This idea is not to be taken in a rigid, dogmatic way; we can certainly acknowledge the general goodness of a person, even if the emphasis of the Christian path is on perfection.

perfect"—and also uttered in private prayer: "I in them and you in me, that they may become perfectly one" (John 17:23 ESV).[5] Christ thus calls us to follow a path toward perfect wholeness. This is a path that cannot be judged according to standards of goodness held by Christians or by the cultures in which they live. Instead, it is a path to be experienced, beyond judgements, through communion with the Living God—the only "One" who *is* good.

Those accustomed to seeing Christianity as a faith that is emphatic on goodness may ask whether perfection—the aim given by Christ—can be pursued through a path centered on goodness precisely. And it can; however, it cannot be reached by it. That is, a path centered on goodness is often motivated by the search for a virtuous security, while the path of perfection demands overcoming the need of security through the pursuit of freedom. A path centered on goodness brings the Christian to a saintly yet bound condition—a comforting type of goodness where there is, eventually, no growth. Growth needs freedom—the freedom that comes through the path of perfection and communion with the Living God. Goodness cannot free us—it can only give us comfort. Freedom is found through the overcoming of fear: one must go beyond comforting goodness to encounter the Truth of God—Love.[6] Hence, goodness without perfection is still bondage—only perfection produces a type of goodness that is not limiting to freedom and growth.

3. Who Is Good?

Jesus said, "Why do you call me good? . . . No one is good—except God alone." Jesus said further, "Be perfect, therefore, as your heavenly Father is perfect."

We are not to call ourselves and others "good," also, because Jesus rejected such a definition on our behalf. Jesus can reject a definition on our behalf because we are human beings and Jesus is the Christ—the Logos incarnate; as the Logos incarnate, he can apprehend the human condition fully, know its nature, and determine what is best for it. By rejecting the

---

5. The NIV reads: "I in them and you in me—so that they may be brought to complete unity." Both translations—"perfectly one" (ESV) and "complete unity" (NIV)—indicate wholeness in communion with God. See the Greek term *teleioō*, "*to be completely organized, to be closely embodied*, Jn. 17:23" (Mounce, *Interlinear New Testament*, 1177).

6. "There is no fear in love. But perfect love drives out fear, because fear has to do with punishment. The one who fears is not made perfect in love" (1 John 4:18).

definition of "good," Jesus chose the best course of action for the human condition, because in doing so, he freed us from the consequences of making an erroneous judgment—the judgment of human nature. The man to whom Jesus replied, "Why do you call me good?" was well-intentioned—he addressed Jesus calling him "good teacher" (Mark 10:17), and Jesus felt love for him;[7] yet, the man's judgment was not adequate. Jesus thus immediately questioned his statement, freeing him from the consequences of his erroneous use of judgment. Also, by replying, "Why do you call me good?" Jesus showed us, by example, how we can free ourselves from the danger of feeling pride when we are called "good" by others. Thus, Jesus' statement, "Why do you call me good?" frees both those who erroneously judge others as good and those who are judged to be good by others.[8]

Yet, some may argue that we should be able to judge who is good, for there are actions, thoughts, and tendencies which are unambiguously not good, as they have "bad"—certainly undesirable—consequences: Should we not know *who* is good if we know *what* is bad? Since God made the human being in his image and similitude and God is good, the essence of human nature is good; hence, regardless of wrong actions, wicked thoughts, and degenerative tendencies, the human being cannot be defined as being—simply—bad (i.e., *what* humans do is not simply *who* they are).[9] Even so, following Christ's words, we see that there are evil people and good people, for he said: "A *good man* brings good things out of the good stored up in him, and an *evil man* brings evil things out of the evil stored up in him" (Matt 12:35, emphasis added); and yet, he continues: "But I tell you that everyone will have to give account on the day of judgment for every empty word they have spoken" (12:36).[10] Therefore, good as absolute goodness—the reality of God, which we cannot judge—differs from good in

---

7. This man was not a hypocrite: "Jesus looked at him and loved him" (Mark 10:21). However, the man could not accept the invitation of Christ to follow him.

8. "I care very little if I am judged by you or by any human court; indeed, I do not even judge myself" (1 Cor 4:3).

9. Since good—as a qualificative for absolute goodness—belongs to God alone, then, there is not a qualificative which opposes good in *reality* (e.g., "bad"); that is, there cannot be an opposing "absolute" to the real Absolute—the real God, the "One" who *is* good.

10. There are no plainly good and plainly evil human beings. But there are *cumulative tendencies*; Jesus said: "You brood of vipers, how can you who are evil say anything good? For the mouth speaks what the heart is full of" (Matt 12:34). See also Matt 7:17–18; 25:21.

comparison[11] to evil—a relative reality we may judge. Nevertheless, we may judge good and evil only under certain circumstances, and cautiously—with the right measure[12]—for both evil and good human beings will be judged, in any case, according to God's judgment.

We are to judge good and evil with the right measure also because the entire human condition is in a stage of learning what good and evil are—by experiencing their consequences.[13] Indeed, the most popular tales tend to be those which illuminate what good and evil are, displaying their effects through relatable narratives; these tales attract our attention because we are ourselves learning what the difference between good and evil is—how it "feels" to reject evil and what kind of growth occurs in such rejection. That is, we do not know what "good" means; instead, we are exploring—discovering—what it means by being exposed to evil, both to its outer manifestations and also to its inner temptations. Just as Jesus was tempted, we are all tempted—tested by evil—so as to discover what goodness is through direct experience.[14] In this sense, a person who follows the path of perfection is not someone who knows "all about" goodness but one whose being rejoices in the alignment with what is good and abhors evil; that is, their being cannot do anything else but reject evil.[15]

---

11. A progressive inquiry into the *nature of evil* reveals several overlapping *stages* in its understanding: evil as the opposite of good; evil in relation to good; evil as the absence of an understanding of reality; evil as the absence of an exploration of reality (i.e., the absence of growth). The understanding of evil as the absence of good, or "privation of the good" (*privatio boni*), has a connotation similar to the last stages.

12. Jesus said: "For in the same way you judge others, you will be judged, and with the measure you use, it will be measured to you" (Matt 7:2). See also Mark 4:24 and Luke 6:38.

13. The eating of the fruit from the tree of knowledge of good and evil by Adam and Eve could signify the beginning of understanding what good and evil are by the human being (i.e., the human being is said to "become like" Elohim, "knowing good and evil" [Gen 3:22]). While in the Garden of Eden, Adam and Eve are infants; after eating the fruit, they acquire a knowledge which seems required in order to eat from the tree of life, so as to become one with Elohim—the divine powers of creation of the Living God—and "live forever" in a new creation. Thus, Adam and Eve are said to be expelled from the Garden of Eden: Are they—humanity or humanness—to grow in their knowledge of good and evil until they acquire enough maturity to eat from the tree of life? Christ, as Logos and Life, shows the path to the tree of life. Augustine, similarly, stated: "The tree of life is the holy of holies, Christ; the tree of the knowledge of good and evil, the will's free choice" (Augustine, *City of God*, 369).

14. Temptation—the testing of faith—is part of the path of perfection. See Jas 1:2–4 (both ESV and NIV).

15. The alignment with what is good is existential; thus, *abhorring evil is an existential*

4. Opposite Culture

Jesus said, "Why do you call me good? . . . No one is good—except God alone." Jesus said further, "Be perfect, therefore, as your heavenly Father is perfect."

In our present culture, people like to think of themselves as being "good but not perfect." Faults of character and behavior are justified accordingly: "I am a good person"; "Everybody makes mistakes"; "I am not perfect"; or, simply, "Nobody is perfect," which attempts to dilute one's own responsibility in an untrue collective judgment. These responses reflect a life orientation opposite to Christ's call to perfection, as they take comfort in imperfection. Such defensive attitudes downgrade the importance of sincere apologizing in society: since "nobody is perfect," then everybody's misdoings are justified—no need to apologize. And because "nobody is perfect," then there are no different grades of perfection but one grade of imperfection—we are all equal in not being perfect. The one thing we shall not be is the one thing Christ told us to be—perfect.

Certainly, Christians have adopted society's understanding of goodness while disregarding perfection (as if it were an unattainable aim). Thus, Christians have widely forgotten the teaching of Christ: *perfection, while living in ignorance of judgment*. Many people think that perfection means being endowed with perfect character and being good according to society's standards; the Christian understanding is just the opposite—aiming for perfection regardless of society's standards, regardless of what others think. Yet, some Christians feel comfortable with the idea of being "good but not perfect" because it does not demand spiritual growth on their part. The statement "I am a good person, but I am not perfect" represents a most convenient belief, especially for those afraid of transformation. How many Christians would say, "I do not know if you and I are good, but let us try to be perfect nevertheless"?[16]

---

rejection—it does not imply the objectivization and analysis of what "good" is, nor does it require knowing "all about" good and evil.

16. This mode of thinking is not new; yet, it is forgotten by many Christians. Augustine, for example, states: "And we indeed recognize in ourselves the image of God, that is, of the supreme Trinity, an image which, though it be not equal to God, or rather, though it be very far removed from Him,—being neither co-eternal, nor, to say all in a word, consubstantial with Him,—is yet nearer to Him in nature than any other of His works, and is destined to be yet restored, that it may bear a still closer resemblance" (Augustine, *City of God*, 483).

While Christ said we shall be perfect, just as the heavenly Father is perfect, some may still argue that to aim for perfection would be presumptuous—an inadequate quest for a humble person, a humble Christian. Thus, they prefer to think of themselves as "good but not perfect" as a sign of virtue and humility. Such Christians assume that they are "good" because they perform their Christian duties (those agreed upon within their Christian community); in contrast, perfection is not their aim, because it is agreed (in their Christian community) to be "too individualistic an affair." Such an attitude may appear to be harmless, yet it can lead to Christian narcissism and religious pride—if one is considered "good" by doing those things which have been agreed upon, then others who do not do such things . . . are they as good as them? Christ's teaching on perfection devastates this type of thinking; it also prevents Christian narcissism in the form of false humility (a widespread form of hypocrisy). Christ's call toward perfection is clear. Hence, humble are those who aim for perfection, because they humble themselves before Christ and his teaching—not before any culture; not before any understanding agreed by a Christian community; not before any convenient philosophy of life.

5. Toward Perfection

Jesus said, "Why do you call me good? . . . No one is good—except God alone." Jesus said further, "Be perfect, therefore, as your heavenly Father is perfect."

There are *three challenges* we will face before entering the path of perfection effectively. Even if preliminary, these challenges are not easy, for they defy the ordinary ways of relating to the world.

First, we will face the challenge of having to go beyond a benevolent and virtuous life (i.e., a righteous life), while not leaving it behind, accepting that perfection belongs to an *order of being* we are not aware of as yet. Jesus said to the young man who called him "good teacher" thus: "If you want to enter life, keep the commandments. . . . 'You shall not murder, you shall not commit adultery, you shall not steal, you shall not give false testimony, honor your father and mother,' and 'love your neighbor as yourself'" (Matt 19:17–19). That is, Jesus advises the man to first keep the moral law. But when the young man replies that he has kept all these commandments and asks, "What do I still lack?" (19:20),[17] Jesus continues: "If you want

17. In other Gospels, the word "lack" is attributed to Jesus, not to the young man:

to be perfect, go, sell your possessions and give to the poor, and you will have treasure in heaven. Then come, follow me" (19:21). Perfection cannot be reached by following the old commandments—the moral law.[18] Only by going beyond a righteous life can we enter the path of perfection; for perfection is not found in safely following a moral law but in Christ—the fulfillment of the law.[19]

Second, we will face the challenge of having to overcome attachment to anything that hinders our path. The young man who called Jesus "good teacher" was well-minded and righteous—he runs up to Jesus, falls on his knees, and asserts that he keeps the moral law of his people. But when he says to Jesus, "What do I still lack?" the young man is immediately tested on his attachment, on what most hinders his path—wealth.[20] He is thus asked to sell his possessions so as to become free in his detachment before following Jesus. But attachment can take many forms: relationships, lifestyles, jobs, routines (or the lack thereof), hobbies, likes (and dislikes), beliefs. In sum: any attachment which comes in the way to perfection will be challenged in entering the path.[21]

"You still lack one thing" (Luke 18:22); "One thing you lack" (Mark 10:21). Here, Jesus does not use the positive affirmation (a call to perfection) but the negative (lacking something); yet, the same outcome—perfection—is implied. Therefore, all three accounts imply the same call: the young man needs something more; following the moral law is not enough to attain perfection, or wholeness, in God.

18. Moral laws, understood as rules of conduct, serve as an initial orientation for the human being; they are necessary to enter the spiritual life, but not enough to attain perfection. However, there is a Moral Being—a moral power—which must come down and be stabilized in the self. The Moral Being rejects sin, granting freedom from deviating and degenerative impulses; it works with the perfection of being in a complementary way. See chapter 5, section 5.

19. "Do not think that I have come to abolish the Law or the Prophets; I have not come to abolish them but to *fulfill* them ... unless your righteousness *surpasses* that of the Pharisees and the teachers of the law, you will certainly not enter the kingdom of heaven" (Matt 5:17–20, emphasis added).

20. Christ's teachings are not normative in terms of behavior; instead, they are invitations to explore existential dispositions (e.g., attachment to wealth, as in the case of the young man). It is the Christ—the Logos apprehending the sentience of each human being—who exposes particular attachments and also determines what is the best path in each case.

21. John of the Cross, in the poem "Para venir a gustarlo todo," states: "To reach that which you do not possess, / you are to go through where you do not possess; / ... / and when you come to fully have it, / wanting nothing you must have it" (Juan de la Cruz, *Obras*, 93, my translation). Spanish original: "para venir a lo que no posees, / has de ir por donde no posees; / ... / y cuando lo vengas del todo a tener, / has de tenerlo sin nada

Third, we will face the last challenge—the call of Christ—which signifies the true entrance to the path. Christ says: "If you want to be perfect... Then come, follow me" (Matt 19:21). That is, if we are to reach perfection, we must follow the Way of Christ—the Way of the Logos made Man. In that leap of faith, we are promised to find a new way of being, perceiving, and relating to the world—in Eternity. To follow Christ means to follow his Way—to receive the Christian mysteries and to truly *listen* to his teachings.[22] To follow Christ also means to cease to follow the world, to stop conforming to the ways and habits of our society, often questioning the culture in which we live.[23] Indeed, aiming for perfection while living in ignorance of judgment implies an *existential stance* that challenges the overly sensorial and mental culture of today.

6. The Nature of Perfection

Jesus said, "Why do you call me good?... No one is good—except God alone." Jesus said further, "Be perfect, therefore, as your heavenly Father is perfect."

Once we have examined the challenges we will face as we enter the path of perfection, we shall further inquire into the nature of perfection. Christ encourages us to follow a path toward perfection, a perfection that can be found in the Father; but he also says that God is the only one who is good. Therefore, the path of perfection implies contemplating perfection

---

querer." Recently, in a similar mystical tradition, María Ángeles Gómez Pascual, in the poem "Entrega," states: "Here you have me, as you wanted: / detached from everything that is sensorial; / free and exempt, alone and stripped, / in this dark night of the senses. / I have nothing, Lord. I ask you for nothing. / I can offer nothing, for I am nothing" (Gómez Pascual, *La piedra y el aire*, 76, my translation). Spanish original: "Aquí me tienes como me has querido: / de todo lo sensible despegada, / libre y exenta, sola y despojada, / en esta oscura noche del sentido. / Nada tengo, Señor. Nada te pido. / Nada puedo ofrecer, pues no soy nada."

22. A similar path is laid out by Symeon: "So I entreat you all, brethren in Christ, first to lay a good foundation *(cf. Heb. 6:1)* of humility as you build up virtues. Then through training in godliness *(1 Tim. 4:7)* raise the house *(cf. Mt. 7:24-25)* of the knowledge of the mysteries of God *(cf. Mt. 13:11; Lk. 8:10)* and so be enlightened by the divine light and see God with the purified eye of the heart *(cf. Mt. 5:8)*, as far as it is possible for us men. Then become initiated more perfectly into the mysteries of the kingdom of heaven *(cf. Mt. 13:11)*" (Symeon the New Theologian, *Discourses*, 345).

23. "Do not conform to the pattern of this world, but be transformed by the renewing of your mind" (Rom 12:2).

as not being centered on goodness. This insight may seem disorienting for those who think that Christian perfection depends on character and behavior—on being welcoming and doing "the right thing."[24] Christ's words imply something different: he urges us to be perfect, as the Father is; therefore, we need to try to comprehend in what sense the Father is perfect, for the Father must have a trait of perfection (different from goodness) that we can attain.

On the same occasion that Christ Jesus said, "Be perfect, therefore, as your heavenly Father is perfect," he also gave indications of how such perfection is to be understood: "You have heard that it was said, 'Love your neighbor and hate your enemy.' But I tell you, love your enemies and pray for those who persecute you" (Matt 5:43–44). That is: the old doctrine established that love for others depends on their qualifications—your neighbor is qualified, but not your enemy. The Way of Christ, however, demands giving oneself to Love—it urges us to consider love for others as free from their qualifications to receive it. Thus, the Love of the New Way does not come out of one's affinities, likings, or friendships but through the recognition of Christ's Being as an operating principle within the self, across all relations. The nature of perfection is, therefore, Love beyond human affections or preferences (affections and preferences that Jesus had as well).[25] By following Christ's invitation to love our enemies, we may feel we are dispossessed of a self we once believed to be true—a self which was dependent on self-love and hate.[26] Indeed, when we pray for our enemies, we do not know ourselves anymore—only Love seems to be known.[27]

24. Character and behavior must be founded in truth and expressed in relation to perfection.

25. "Love your enemies" does not mean to feel affection for them; affection is built on relationships, and we cannot feel affection for everybody, or in the same way for each person we know or meet. Jesus also had individual affections—was not John particularly "loved" by Jesus (John 13:23; 19:26; 20:2), even though Jesus loved all his disciples greatly in an affectionate way?

26. There is a "who" or "I" that remains, but the self—as facade—falls away. I have argued that the "I" remains after the realization of God: "Having gone myself through classical 'I'-deaths and self-dissolution experiences, still, I recognize the fundamental 'I' and all the aspects of being necessary to human life" (Portilla, *Spiritual Experience*, 207).

27. The process of acknowledging God's Love by self-dispossession (in prayer for our enemies, and contemplation) at some stages may show similarities with the approaching of God by negation of self (*via negativa*). As an example, John of the Cross, in the poem "Para venir a gustarlo todo," states: "To wholly come to the Whole [God], / you are to deny yourself wholly—in all" (Juan de la Cruz, *Obras*, 93, my translation). Spanish original: "para venir del todo al todo, / has de negarte del todo en todo."

A further indication to understand the nature of perfection is Christ's description of the Father's Love: "He causes his sun to rise on the evil and the good, and sends rain on the righteous and the unrighteous" (Matt 5:45). Therefore, by following the teaching of Christ, we reach the perfection of the Father when our being reflects Divine Love toward friend and enemy, evil and good, the righteous and the unrighteous. Christ's teaching suggests a Love that functions like the sun and nourishes like the rain. Thus, to love means to shine and to nourish; and to nourish means to give Life, and to know that the Spirit is the living water of eternal life. Love, and not goodness, is the trait of the Father which Christ urges us to acquire; we shall aspire to it so as to become perfect—just like him.

7. Living in the Light of Truth

Jesus said, "Why do you call me good? . . . No one is good—except God alone." Jesus said further, "Be perfect, therefore, as your heavenly Father is perfect."

We have discussed the three challenges we will face at the beginning of the path of perfection—aiming beyond goodness and moral law, overcoming attachment, and following Christ and his Way. We also discerned what the nature of Christian perfection is—Love that is not conditioned by the object of love. Yet, how do we know that we have reached perfection?[28] The answer to this question is in the testimony of those who have followed the path themselves: perfection is fulfilled in the experience of transfiguration in the Light, the embodied manifestation of the Light of being.[29] By

---

28. We are looking for an indication while being alive, for perfection can be attained while living, even if another type of perfection awaits beyond. Thus, the indication of perfection cannot be the Resurrection, as that would be an impossibility while living, at least in our present condition. Also, perfection cannot be physical untouchability or immortality, as Christ Jesus passed through the Passion and died, being already perfect, like the Father. Further, we are *not* looking for the "signs" of the Spirit or the kingdom (healings, etc.) but trying to understand the perfection of the Father.

29. The testimonies of transfiguration in the Light can take various forms, depending on the times and context. Byzantine Christian monk Symeon the New Theologian recounts his own experience: "I fell prostrate on the ground, and at once I saw, and behold, a great light was immaterially shining on me and seized hold of my whole mind and soul, so that I was struck with amazement at the unexpected marvel and I was, as it were, in ecstasy . . . 'Whether I was in the body, or outside the body' *(2 Cor. 12:2, 3)*, I conversed with this Light. The Light itself knows it . . . It expelled from me all material denseness and bodily heaviness that made my members to be sluggish and numb . . . Thus all the

being conscious of the Father (thus living in the Father), our nature, regenerated by Christ, starts reflecting the luminous powers of the Logos—the Light birthed in the Father as the Son, which shines perfectly and nourishes perfectly, thus giving Life like the sun. Such a phenomenon is the fulfilling manifestation of what we call Love, which is the nature of perfection, as we have seen. Perfection is thus attained when the realization of the Father—the Source of all existence—is accompanied by the transfiguration of the Christian in the Light. Christ's teachings indicate such a possibility precisely: "When your eyes are healthy, your whole body also is full of light" (Luke 11:34); "Therefore, if your whole body is full of light, and no part of it dark, it will be just as full of light as when a lamp shines its light on you" (11:36). The capacity of transfiguration in the Light manifests itself in those who follow Christ's call to be perfect, displaying different luminous qualities and degrees of intensity of the Christ Light according to each person's characteristics.[30]

---

perceptions of my mind and my soul were wholly concentrated on the ineffable joy of that Light" (Symeon the New Theologian, *Discourses*, 200–201, 198). (Testimony recounted by Symeon, and attributed to him as his actual experience by Nicetas Stethatos, the biographer of Symeon.) More recently, Marc Chaduc testified of his own and Benedictine Henri Le Saux's transfigurations: "A sudden and overwhelming vision of *param jyotir*, of the Great Light, for three hours; engulfing the total depths of myself, in the ineffable light which I am. An experience of annihilating, beatifying death, an awakening to the Self! At the same time I had the definitive revelation that Henri (Le Saux) is my guru.* I saw him in his blinding glory, transfigured in the Light" (Odette Baumer-Despeigne, "The Spiritual Way of Henri Le Saux, Swami Abhishiktananda," 22, qtd. in du Boulay, *Cave of the Heart*, 224). *Chaduc uses Hindu-yogic terminology because he was living in India in times of deep interreligious/interfaith Hindu-Christian dialogue. For a patristic-theological explanation of these experiences, see Gregory Palamas's "D. Deification in Christ," in Palamas, *Triads*, 57–69.

30. While transfiguration in the Light is possible for all those who follow the path of perfection to its end, there are gradations in the Light manifesting itself in the perfection of the Father. Symeon states: "Let no one deceive you! God is light (1 John 1:5), and to those who have entered into union with Him He imparts of His own brightness to the extent that they have been purified" (Symeon the New Theologian, *Discourses*, 195). I have attested to this view when describing my path: "Sometimes, it would be a spontaneous and gentle recognition of the Light within the self; other times, an intense experience which would challenge the limitations of my physicality. In some occasions, such personal Light could be so radiant that I would not be able to see anything but Conscious Light" (Portilla, *Spiritual Experience*, 73). Thus, to be perfect, as the Father is perfect, implies an unbounded unconditional stance on inclusive Love. Yet, *perfection allows diversity and difference,* for there are gradations of manifestation of the Light of being due to various factors. For example: the capacity of Light manifestation; the spiritual nature; the soul's characteristics; the mind's purity; the spiritual relationship

Remembering that the nature of perfection is Love is difficult in our societies. Even if we come to abide existentially in the Father and to experience the Light of being, the culturally misplaced understanding of perfection affects us. Certainly, the experience of God does not make us fully immune to society's attitudes and pressures, for we cannot completely isolate ourselves from the societal context in which we live. Our societies ask us for perfection of function, *not* giving value to *how* we perform those functions and *how we exist*. We are not asked to be perfect, yet perfect results are demanded of us. Such a demand hinders the remembrance of our commitment to Love (the true nature of perfection). Some Christians find comfort embracing the idea of perfection of function while they are *still* successful and praised in a society with ever-increasing demands. But we shall remember that Christian perfection is to Love as the Father; it does not depend on the opinions of society and its demands. In fact, society demands the perfection of function and consents to imperfection in the Spirit, while the Christian is called to do the opposite—to follow the path of spiritual perfection while accepting, gladly and compassionately, dysfunctionality regarding society's demands.[31]

To fully accept and embody the profundity and vastness of heart Christ's call to perfection implies, we must develop a view of reality that can be understood as mature innocence. Just before the conversation with the wealthy young man, Christ welcomed a group of children and blessed them, saying: "Let the little children come to me, and do not hinder them, for the kingdom of God belongs to such as these. Truly I tell you, anyone who will not receive the kingdom of God like a little child will never enter it" (Mark 10:14–15).[32] To become aware of the living kingdom, we must see the world through a childlike innocence at heart, so that God can be realized in our being and the Spirit can work effectively in us. It is our willingness to rightly look and receive, to spiritually hear and embody, in a way long forgotten yet alive in us,[33] that will make us realize the teaching

---

with the person one encounters in contemplation (in the case of encounters in the Light with another person).

31. By accepting dysfunctionality, I do not mean to give a pass to "willing dysfunctionality"—the lack of any responsibility or willingness to do the best work possible—but to recognize the value of the person as a whole, truly apprehending the person's quality, intention, and presence; in sum: the contribution of *mere being*.

32. See also Luke 18:16–17.

33. The expression "forgotten yet alive" refers to an originally more vital and inspiriting Christianity, as it is recovered in our day and age.

of Christ on Earth. The apparent toughness of Christ's teaching—no one is good, but we ought to be perfect—is thus transformed, through an innocent heart, in the vast reality of being it represents.

Truth

Jesus said, "No one is good—except God alone," yet also "Be perfect, therefore, as your heavenly Father is perfect." When our hope for another person lies in goodness, we demand an impossible feat; when it lies in perfection (in Christ's sense), we wish them to attain a real possibility. To follow Christ means to explore a New Life with others and to find out its manifold forms of expression in the perfection we are called to pursue—as Love. Christ would never load us with unreachable aims but rather give us the only freedom that is real—now and everlastingly—the truth.

CHAPTER 3

Destroy This Temple
The Unbreakable Real Church

1. Who Understands?

JESUS SAID: "DESTROY THIS temple, and I will raise it again in three days" (John 2:19)[1]—"But the temple he had spoken of was his body" (2:21).

When Christ voiced this statement, nobody understood him: not his detractors, not the multitudes, not his disciples (who were to mourn his death for three days). Christ did not explain this saying. And it spread among the people and fueled the anger against him up to his trial and death on the cross. In his trial, before the Sanhedrin, his accusers misquoted him: "We heard him say, 'I will destroy this temple made with human hands and in three days will build another, not made with hands'" (Mark 14:58);[2] yet,

---

1. This statement of Christ belongs to the first cleansing of the temple as it is described in the Gospel of John. There was at least one more episode of the same nature, for the descriptions in the other Gospels are different and occurred later in Christ's Office—after the triumphal entry into Jerusalem; see Matt 21:12–17; Mark 11:15–19; Luke 19:45–48. *Hermeneutical note*: the double cleansing of the temple is a reading welcomed by the church fathers—John Chrysostom, for example (see Gillquist, *Orthodox Study Bible*, 216).

2. See Matthew as well: "This fellow said, 'I am able to destroy the temple of God and rebuild it in three days'" (Matt 26:61). It seems that at some point, the chief priests and the Pharisees knew that Jesus could be referring to his body, for in order to convince Pilate to guard the tomb after his death, they quoted Christ as follows: "After three days I will rise again" (Matt 27:63).

he kept silent.³ And on the cross, even then, he was mocked because of this saying: "You who are going to destroy the temple and build it in three days, save yourself!" (Matt 27:40).⁴ Jesus never explained this saying—his Resurrection did it for him. Then, the risen Christ spoke: "Thus it is written, and thus it was necessary for the Christ to suffer and to rise from the dead the third day" (Luke 24:46 NKJV).⁵

2. Authority Is Christ's Body

Jesus said: "Destroy this temple, and I will raise it again in three days"— "But the temple he had spoken of was his body."

Christ entered the temple of Jerusalem, and seeing the commercial activities carried on in it, he raged. He raged because he cared.⁶ Jesus took some cords, made a whip, and stormed against what he considered an abomination worthy of violent action.⁷ "Take these things away; do not make my Father's house a house of trade" (John 2:16 ESV), he said to those who sold doves. Thus, clearly and openly, Christ Jesus cared for the Jewish temple—for its functional power as the house of God (the Father, his Father⁸) and for the sacredness of its space and premises. That Jesus embodied a New Way⁹ and, consequently, was often critical of the doctrines of

---

3. Mark 14:60–61. *Silence* is Jesus' reply to the lack of understanding of those who despised him and had plotted to kill him; *they already had condemned him* regardless of any word he could say. Indeed, Nicodemus, a Pharisee, had visited Jesus to discuss his teachings, for they knew he was "a teacher come from God" (John 3:1–21 ESV); further, in an occasion before the trial, Nicodemus had pointed out to the chief priests and other Pharisees *not* to judge Jesus without hearing from him in person, and he had been reprimanded for it (John 7:50–52). See the passage of Philip and the Ethiopian in Acts 8:26–40: "He was led like a sheep to the slaughter, as *a lamb* before its shearer is *silent*, so he did not open his mouth" (8:32, emphasis added).

4. See also Mark 15:28–30.

5. It was only then that the disciples understood him: "And He opened their understanding, that they might comprehend the Scriptures" (Luke 24:45 NKJV). See also John 2:22.

6. "Zeal for your house will consume me" (John 2:17), his disciples recalled (see Ps 69:9).

7. A *hermeneutics of freedom* does not support prescriptive actions but rather existential freedom—in the Spirit.

8. Even as a boy, Jesus had identified the temple as *the house of his Father*: "Didn't you know I had to be in my Father's house?" (Luke 2:49).

9. See chapter 6, section 3, on the New Worship. See also Stephen's defense—"However,

the Jewish leaders did not make him debunk the Jewish faith or disregard its holy places: he cared for the Jewish faith and preached within the Jewish holy places, for he was the foretold Messiah.

The Temple Event[10] was as much a reproach to the merchants as it was to the Jewish leaders for consenting to such activities. Indeed, Jesus' authority to take such a fierce action was immediately questioned by them: "What sign can you show us to prove your authority to do all this?" (John 2:18). Jesus replied: "Destroy this temple, and I will raise it again in three days" (2:19). Such was Christ Jesus' answer to the question on his authority; no further explanation was given. "It has taken forty-six years to build this temple, and you are going to raise it in three days?" (2:20), they further said to him. Yet, Christ's answer was accurate and true: Christ had authority to expel the merchants and the money changers from the human-made house of God (the Father, his Father), because Christ's body is the God-made temple of the Living Spirit.[11] Thus, Christ's authority is his body.

Christ's reply regarding his authority challenges the belief that the religious, economic, and political domains (in his time represented by the Jewish authorities, the merchants, and the Roman rulers,[12] respectively) are the highest authority. The Temple Event is a reminder of the order of society necessary for Divine Life: the divine domain has authority over all

---

the Most High does not live in houses made by human hands. As the prophet says: 'Heaven is my throne, and the earth is my footstool. What kind of house will you build for me? says the Lord. Or where will my resting place be? Has not my hand made all these things?'" (Acts 7:48–50). If we put together both Jesus' take on the temple as his Father's house and his New Way and New Worship—transcending any human-made temple ("You will worship the Father neither on this mountain nor in Jerusalem. . . . the true worshipers will worship the Father *in* the Spirit and *in* truth" [John 4:21–23, emphasis added])—we may reach the following conclusion: the temple is important in the times of Christ Jesus' Incarnation, but when the Office of Christ was accomplished (with the coming of the Fire of Life at Pentecost), the New Worship was fully and effectively inaugurated, and Stephen's defense is consistent with it. Paul seems to follow a similar argument (Acts 17:24).

10. I use the term "Temple Event" to describe the first of any number of episodes of similar characteristics which are commonly known as the cleansing of the temple (see prior note at the beginning of the chapter).

11. Christ has life in himself (John 1:4; 5:26; 11:25), but also the Spirit descends on him and dwells in him (Matt 3:16–17; Mark 1:10–11; Luke 3:22; John 1:32), and the Father is in him (John 10:38; 14:10, 11; 17:21, 23). And so, Christ can say that *he will raise* his bodily temple, because he has life in himself, as the Father has.

12. The Temple Event could be interpreted as having implications beyond the Jewish community—as a disruption of the economic culture and agreed upon customs of trade under the Roman rule.

domains; the religious, economic, and political powers are never alone and above all else; they must be servants of the whole and know their place in society (religion must be reliable, economics economical, and politics polite). Otherwise, they are to be challenged—by divine descent, in this occasion by the Son of God. Upon the Resurrection, Christ's body became "the firstfruits" of Divine Life on Earth (1 Cor 15:20–23), a Life in which the religious, economic, and political domains are to be transformed under his authority.

3. The Bodily Temple

Jesus said: "Destroy this temple, and I will raise it again in three days"—"But the temple he had spoken of was his body."

Christ spoke of his body as a "temple," but the differences between a temple made of stone and the human body are many. Stone-made temples may hold power—their location, their architecture, the rituals of consecration and ceremonies performed in them, the prayers of the faithful, and even the objects they hold (relics, art, books, etc.) are reasons for it; further, their symbolic meaning within a given community, city, or geographical context plays a part in their significance. The human body is capable of holding power as well, but also of refining it and expressing it to a greater extent through the participation of consciousness and sentience—reflecting a more fulfilling Light.[13] Certainly, it is the human being who is created in the image and similitude of God, not stone-made temples inexistent both at the beginning and at the end of time—there are no temples either in Eden or in the New Jerusalem.[14] Thus, the human body is more qualified than any temple to reflect God's Light—it is a "who" (like God), not an "it." For this reason, individuals who perceive and embody the Light of God bring people to God better than any temple.

In order to understand how we may experience the body as the temple of the Living Spirit, we must first examine our ways of thinking about the body. The body, as we usually know it, is only an idea based on a belief—that sensorial perceptions are the best way to define what the body is. That is, we believe that our body is a body of flesh which we can see; it has precise limitations (i.e., skin that we can touch). We may further think of our body

---

13. Gregory Palamas states: "The eternal glory of God *is* participable, for that which in God is visible in some way, is also participable" (Palamas, *Triads*, 99).

14. Rev 21:22–23.

as consisting of bones, muscles, organs, and glands, because we experience these bodily aspects when we have problems with them—through pain. Thus, a broken bone, a muscle cramp, stomach discomfort, etc., are ways of experiencing—and so, of conceiving of—the body. Pleasure also shows another dimension of bodily consciousness—through food, sexuality, dance, music, or visual arts.[15] But none of these perceptions, including pain and pleasure, shows us what the body is in reality—the temple of God. The question which follows is this: Are there other *means of experience* through which we may apprehend the body as the temple of the Living Spirit?

We know that "man became a living being" when God "breathed into his nostrils the breath of life" (Gen 2:7); we also know that the risen Christ breathed on his disciples the Holy Spirit.[16] Thus, *breath* is the beginning of life, and also of the New Life—the Spirit gives itself through breath, as Life.[17] Hence, breath is not just a physical function but, more fundamentally, the pulse of existence, the rhythm of the Spirit coming into being. In fact, through spiritual exercises that involve breathing, we can verify that the body is animated by Spirit (these exercises have been used in monastic practice and are often given to beginners in the path of discipleship).[18] Yet further, the Christian Way gives specific means to apprehend the body as the temple of God: the Spiritual Force that descends upon Baptism makes our body a receptacle of God's operating power—a tangible presence which we can feel; the sanctified bread and wine infuse our bodily awareness with Christ's awareness of his body (thus, we become one with the Body of Christ); the sanctification given by the Pentecostal Fire fosters our participation in a process of regeneration so that the Christ Light may be expressed through us. The Christian mysteries are thus the means for our

---

15. "Pleasure" can also be part of the soul's realm, but here the inquiry is centered on the body.

16. John 20:22.

17. The Greeks used the same word for breath and Spirit: *pneuma*. In the Old Testament, the words for breath and Spirit are connected: "As long as my breath is in me, and the spirit of God is in my nostrils" (Job 27:3 ESV). In various languages, the words for breath and Spirit are quite similar; for example: *respiración* and *espíritu* (Spanish, a Latin language); d[u]h (*u* as in "umbrella") and *duh* (Bulgarian, a Slavic language).

18. Spiritual breathing exercises were certainly known before Christ; various faith traditions—Hinduism, Buddhism, Taoism—utilized breathing exercises and understood the connection between the breath, Spirit, and Life. Also, within Christianity, some monastic traditions have used breathing exercises; for example, within the Hesychast tradition, masters such as Ps.-Symeon and Nicephorus taught these methods (see Palamas, *Triads*, 45–46, 127n50).

consciousness to be able to apprehend our body as the temple of God—in a Christ-like manner.

4. The Church of the Called

Jesus said: "Destroy this temple, and I will raise it again in three days"— "But the temple he had spoken of was his body."

Jesus introduced the idea of his church while being among his disciples. At some point, there was a debate on who Jesus really was: "Some say John the Baptist; others say Elijah; and still others, Jeremiah or one of the prophets" (Matt 16:14). And so, he asked: "But what about you? ... Who do you say I am?" (16:15). Then promptly, Simon Peter replied: "You are the Christ, the Son of the living God" (16:16 ESV);[19] and Jesus said, "Blessed are you, Simon son of Jonah, for this was not revealed to you by flesh and blood, but by my Father in heaven. And I tell you that you are Peter, and on this rock I will build my church" (16:17–18).[20] These words of Christ give us important insights into the understanding of his church.

First, Jesus restates the names "Simon" (which means "to listen") and "Peter" (which comes from "rock").[21] The use of these two names (not just the latter) may be relevant in that it portrays the importance of both listening and rocklike faith for those who are following the Way of Christ. Hence, through *right listening*, one becomes fitted to "hear"[22] the revelation of the Father—that Jesus is "the Christ, the Son of the living God." This revelation becomes the foundation of the Christian faith—an existential conviction *firm as a rock* on which Christ is to build his church.

---

19. See also Mark 8:27–30; Luke 9:18–20. This revelation occurred among Jesus' closest and more trusted disciples. "Then he ordered his disciples not to tell anyone that he was the Messiah" (Matt 16:20).

20. *Methodological note*: part of the current biblical exegesis argues the concept *ekklēsia* ("church") as being different from Jesus' ideas, even suggesting that this passage of Scripture may have been an insertion of the evangelist to accommodate early Christian organizational developments into the narrative of the Gospel, hence not an actual saying of Jesus (see Pesce, *De Jesús*, 364–68). This book, however, does not question any passage of Scripture; if it arrives at similar conclusions regarding the ideas of Jesus, it does so through a *hermeneutics of freedom* and an inquiry on the meaning of *ekklēsia* (see below).

21. Jesus had changed the name of Simon to Cephas when Simon's brother, Andrew, introduced him to Jesus: "Jesus looked at him and said, 'You are Simon son of John. You will be called Cephas' (which, when translated, is Peter)" (John 1:42).

22. Matt 11:15; Mark 4:9; 4:23; Luke 14:35. Without *right hearing*, there is no understanding and no right path, and no discipleship is possible.

Second, the meaning of church is community but, more specifically, the gathering of those who are called.[23] Thus, the church of Christ is the *gathering of the called*—those whose ears can hear and follow his call. Simon Peter (the one who "listens" and is firm like a "rock" on what he listens) and his brother Andrew (the one who is "strong" and "brave") both heard and followed the call of Jesus: "Follow me, and I will make you fishers of men" (Matt 4:19 ESV).[24] Likewise, Christians are to listen and follow Christ's call. And so, the saying "on this rock I will build my church" may be understood thus: upon the faith that Christ Jesus is the Son of the Living God the communion of the called—the real church—will be established.

Hence, the real church[25] is experienced in the communion of the called; it is formed by the called and sustained by the called, with Christ at its center. The magnitude of the real church—the church which Christ called "my church"—is only known to Christ. It includes both individuals who live in the physical world and those who have passed and await in Eternity. Those who live in the physical world become agents of the real church when they know their bodies as Christ knew his body—as the sentient, God-made temple of the Living Spirit. They are consciously part of the Body of Christ, which is comprised of all Christians in whom the Light of Christ is bestowed and lives.[26]

The word "church," of course, is not used only in reference to the real church: there are temple churches and there are institutional churches together with the real church.[27] Temple churches and institutional churches

---

23. Nowadays, the word "church" is commonly understood in reference to a formal spiritual community—a congregation, a group formed by the faithful, a coming together because of a common faith and set of beliefs, with a formal institutional connotation. I use the composite meanings of the Greek *ekklēsia/n* (Matt 16:18) to understand the real church as *the communion of the called*—the coming together of those called out from wherever they were, whichever was their way of life, to the Way of Christ.

24. The call of Peter and Andrew by Jesus (Matt 4:19) would had taken place sometime after their first meeting when Andrew introduced Simon to Jesus and Jesus changed Simon's name to Cephas (i.e., Peter) (John 1:42). It is thus likely (and reasonable) that *the call of the disciples* happened when they knew Jesus already; upon his call, their common journey began and he started to preach (Matt 4:12–22).

25. On the "real church," see also section 7.

26. "Now you are the body of Christ, and each one of you is a part of it" (1 Cor 12:27).

27. In this inquiry, I do not discuss Christian denominations, even when they use the word "church" to define themselves. Thus, the institutional church is not equivalent to any Christian denomination (see section 6). These distinctions are crucial in the application of a *hermeneutics of freedom*, which frees the word "church" by clarifying the different forces associated with it.

are real, but they are not real in the same sense as the real church, for they are not eternal and do not represent all the called by Christ. That is, the temple church and the institutional church have a function in Christianity, past and present; but they are not the eternal and thus truly real church, which may be formed by members of various Christian denominations, and nonmembers as well—individuals known to Christ only. The real church is a temple-less, institution-less, communion-based church; it is as the New Jerusalem, where there are no temples or institutions, but God and Lamb alone,[28] Consciousness and Light alone. That Christians may know the difference between the temple church, the institutional church, and the real church (and the position of their Christian denomination in regard to them) does not mean that they are mindful of such differences when they use the word "church." In fact, the word "church" hardly ever signifies what Jesus referred to anymore. Thus, the real church of Christ—the *gathering of the called*—has become the forgotten church. However: forgotten to the world—not to Christ.

5. The Temple Church

Jesus said: "Destroy this temple, and I will raise it again in three days"—"But the temple he had spoken of was his body."

Some Christians trust that they are on good terms with God only because they go to a temple church regularly; God's "approval" is thought to be in the temple—by *the mere act of going* to it. Thinking in this way, Christians soon forget that the temple of the Living Spirit is their body. The transformative path of Christian contemplation—the cultivation of the awareness of the Christ Light within one's own body and being—is thus substituted by a routine: temple practice, with doubtful transformative effects. Going to the temple church hence becomes an occasion for self-justification and social amusement rather than an opportunity to connect with the real church through the power of the temple. Indeed, gatherings at temple churches often create conditions leading to religious pride and the arrogant exclusion of those who practice differently.[29] Thus, temple church practice tends

---

28. "I did not see a temple in the city [New Jerusalem], because the Lord God Almighty and the Lamb are its temple. The city does not need the sun or the moon to shine on it, for the glory of God gives it light, and the Lamb is its lamp" (Rev 21:22–23). See also Rev 21:24–27; 22:1–5.

29. Jesus told John *not* to exclude others or limit the actions of others: "For no one

to replicate patterns of behavior that Jesus criticized: "You are the ones who justify yourselves in the eyes of others, but God knows your hearts. What people value highly is detestable in God's sight" (Luke 16:15).

The temple church is not a problem; but self-justification, religious pride, and hypocrisy, which derive from temple-church malpractice, are problems (quite serious for Christ). Certainly, Christ Jesus considered the Jewish temple to be the house of God (the Father). For Jesus, the problem was not the temple but the use of the temple and the hypocrisy of those who ruled the temple. The challenge to hypocrisy was central to Christ Jesus' public ministry;[30] thus, it should be central to Christian practice as well.[31] If we ask how we are to prevent temple-church malpractice, the answer is simple: in the Temple Event, we see that Jesus had the authority to criticize the use of the temple's premises and the hypocrisy displayed by the Jewish leaders because *he knew* that his body was the temple of the Living Spirit; therefore, temple-church practice ceases to be a problem when the Christian realizes that their body is the temple of the Living Spirit. Hence, Christians who worship in temple churches can prevent self-justification, religious pride, and hypocrisy by locating the center of their practice not in the temple church but in the bodily human temple, in communion with the real church. In fact, temple-church practice is meant to reveal and remind the Christian that the true temple is their body and that the real church is

---

who does a miracle in my name can in the next moment say anything bad about me, for whoever is not against us is for us" (Mark 9:39–40). Yet, Christian gatherings at times follow an opposite tendency—exclusionism and criticizing the doings of others; it might well be a general religious tendency, but Christians should be particularly mindful of this issue if they are to follow Christ's Way. See also Luke 9:50.

30. Christ Jesus heavily criticized those in power—the teachers of the law and the Pharisees. Jesus advises the people: "So you must be careful to do everything they tell you. But do not do what they do, for they do not practice what they preach" (Matt 23:3). See the warnings against hypocrisy (Matt 23:1–12; also 12:14–16; Luke 12:1–12; 20:45–47; Mark 12:38), the seven woes (Matt 23:13–39), and the six woes at the table (Luke 11:37–53).

31. Based on several types of hypocrisy, Christ Jesus gave good advice on how to practice properly: (a) in *giving*—"Be careful not to practice your righteousness in front of others to be seen by them" (Matt 6:1–5; see also Mark 12:41–44); (b) in *prayer*—"And when you pray, do not be like the hypocrites, for they love to pray standing in the synagogues and on the street corners to be seen by others. . . . But when you pray, go into your room, close the door and pray to your Father, who is unseen" (Matt 6:5–8); (c) in *fasting*—"When you fast, do not look somber as the hypocrites do . . . . put oil on your head and wash your face, so that it will not be obvious to others that you are fasting" (Matt 6:16–18).

not the walled temple in which they pray; in prayer, the divine awe in the communion with the called transcends physical limitations.

Anytime the body is not thought of as the foundational temple of the Living Spirit, a reconsideration of the importance of the temple church becomes urgent. The temple church is not inherently necessary to the practice of Christianity: Jesus and his disciples practiced without temples; most early Christians practiced without temples for three centuries after;[32] many Christians today organize their gatherings out of temples as well. The Christian can break away from the belief that the temple is where God mainly resides (a temple made by human hands). Attention and consciousness must be grounded in the body, which was made by God in his similitude. The challenge lies not in determining whether temple-church practice is beneficial (for some it is) but in conceiving of a serious Christianity for which temple-church practice (and, in general, worship tied to a particular location and place) is optional. The challenge to the need of a location and place for worship was presented quite clearly by Jesus to the Samaritan woman: "Woman . . . believe me, a time is coming when you will worship the Father neither on this mountain nor in Jerusalem. . . . Yet a time is coming and has now come when the true worshipers will worship the Father *in* the Spirit and *in* truth, for they are the kind of worshipers the Father seeks. God is spirit, and his worshipers must worship *in* the Spirit and *in* truth" (John 4:21–24, emphasis added).[33]

6. The Institutional Church

Jesus said: "Destroy this temple, and I will raise it again in three days"— "But the temple he had spoken of was his body."

Jesus did not teach any fixed dogma; he never exposed a definitive set of instructions; he never established an organization based on agreed upon codes of conduct. Instead, he—in communion with the Spirit and the Father—inspired a living understanding of Divine Existence, often challenging the ways and doctrines promulgated by the religious authorities of his time. Each individual was thus free—endowed with responsibility—to live the New Way as a process of discovery and continuous transformation. The same disposition should be encouraged today: shared beliefs in Christian

---

32. Early Christians gathered at homes (Acts 2:46; 20:20; 1 Cor 16:19), Jewish places of worship (Acts 19:8), and other functional spaces.

33. Chapter 6, section 3 focuses on this passage.

gatherings should not rule out each individual's capacity of discernment and right to dissent; every Christian should pursue their path with a clear conscience in their accountability. Christian gatherings and communities, however, tend to display a problematic pattern to this end: beliefs start substituting faith; the individual's capacity of discernment fades away; the real church is forgotten. The institutional church, being a force influencing many of these gatherings and communities, is to be mindful of it.

The institutional church is not the real church. The institutional church[34] is a construction of collective consciousness; the real church is the power of Christ and (all) the called by him. The institutional church represents a historical process—of human beings, mostly men,[35] in their struggle to conciliate the social, political, religious, and divine domains. In such a process, one individual alone has very little importance and enjoys little freedom. On the other hand, the real church is a meta-community of free individuals, free from gender concerns,[36] who rejoice by being in communion with Christ and working for the emergence of Divine Life.[37] Hence, the institutional church has difficulties with being aligned with the real church (i.e., with being transparent to it)[38] because the real church cherishes the individual—Christ knows his own—while the institutional church cherishes the collective first and only later negotiates how individuals fit in; being so, the institutional church often has difficulties embracing later-to-be-proclaimed "saints." The institutional church is not a system, but it can become a system; it is thus the role of the faithful of any Christian

---

34. The term "institutional church" does *not* refer to any Christian denomination in particular. That is, I do *not* consider Christian denominations equivalent to the institutional church. Any Christian, and so any Christian denomination, has to deal with the realities of the institutional church, the temple church, and the real church. What I present in this chapter is an exploration of these realities through a *hermeneutics of freedom*. It is up to each Christian and Christian denomination to explore how they relate to, represent, or feel identified with these realities.

35. This is a critique, not that it ought to be so.

36. In line with the Resurrection (Matt 22:30; Mark 12:25). Christ Jesus exemplified freedom from gender concerns; for example, he revealed the New Worship and his identity as Messiah to a Samaritan woman (John 4).

37. Christ Jesus said: "For where two or three gather in my name, there am I with them" (Matt 18:20). Christian gatherings may start as a sincere existential encounter of two or three individuals who are called by and in Christ; thus, the nucleus of any Christian collective aligned with the real church lies in the meeting of two or three individuals. Numbers are not important but rather the quality of the individuals.

38. The ideal for the institutional church is to be aligned as much as possible with the real church; greater alignment implies greater transparency.

denomination to prevent the institutional church from becoming an "it"—a system which operates as if removed from Love, making its members obey rules and conform with the dominant aim of protecting itself.[39] Indeed, the first warning of Christ to the churches is the following: "Yet I hold this against you: You have forsaken the love you had at first" (Rev 2:4).

In some parts of the modern world, the institutional church seems weaker than in the past;[40] but weaker does not mean worse (nor that Christianity is in decline). That is, some Christians think Christianity is fading because in their countries, the institutional church has less influence in the life of society.[41] But such changes do not affect the real church, for what is eternal cannot fade away. Additionally, the current challenges can bring Christians closer to the real church. Christianity, now as ever, needs to be represented not by Christians who seek security in a powerful institutional church but by Christians who find confirmation in Christ's Being. The weakening of the institutional church presents an opportunity for Christians to reconsider their ways and priorities, to remember their purpose, to commit in their aid to a living understanding of Christianity, nowadays rediscovered in open societies where institutional forces do not suppress the individual's growth.

7. The Unknown (Real) Church

Jesus said: "Destroy this temple, and I will raise it again in three days"— "But the temple he had spoken of was his body."

Christian solitude—the figure of a solitary Christian—is as valid as that of the Christian community. The desert and the hermitage are as valid as the temple. And we can all find a desert-like landscape in our

---

39. Theologian Stanley Hauerwas states: "I fear that much of the Christianity that surrounds us assumes our task is to save appearances by protecting God from Job-like anguish. But if God is the God of Jesus Christ, then God does not need our protection. What God demands is not protection, but truth" (Hauerwas, *Hannah's Child*, chap. 5 ["Catholics"]).

40. Some reasons for it are: the separation of the political domain from religious sanction; cultural secularization; the discredit of some Christian denominations due to abuse/malpractice; the incapability of Christian denominations to meet the standards of inclusivity in complex, heterogeneous societies; a wider offering of psychological and spiritual counseling alternative/complementary to Christian guidance; the resistance of Christian denominations to changing doctrine when necessary.

41. Each country's circumstances are different; also, there are important differences between the Global South and the Global North. But this is not a topic discussed here.

surroundings, or a hermitage-like corner in our homes, to pray and meditate. Christ said: "When you pray, go into your room and shut the door and pray to your Father who is in secret. And your Father who sees in secret will reward you" (Matt 6:6 ESV).[42] Christianity is not to be chiefly defined by the visible community—one formed by institutions and human gatherings in temple churches; it is the "invisible"—ungraspable—community that represents the existential power of the church—the real church.[43] The Christian who prays, meditates, and contemplates in solitude (thus following Christ's teaching of secret prayer) is not alone: through solitary prayer, they connect with the sentience of humanity, with all their brothers and sisters in Christ, and also with the invisible hosts of divine beings. This connection is possible because prayer and contemplation bring the Christian to the discovery of their self in a reality without the habitual boundaries; for there is an interior which is egoless, and its realization breaks through self-isolating constructs, penetrating the mental and physical walls that separate Christians from each other. Solitary devout Christians are not alone but in communion with the real church; their vision and understanding of Christianity is broad—different from that of Christians who sit in temple churches thinking "the church" is just what they can see.

The magnitude of the real church is known to Christ and unknown to Christians—we cannot know the vastness of the real church, for that would mean having the capacity to know all the called by Christ throughout history. In that sense, the real church is very different from any temple-church community or institutional church: church communities are formed by individuals who are known to each other; the real church, by individuals who are known to Christ (such is the foundation). Comparably, the institutional church is formed by individuals who organize themselves to work for Christ, meeting physically when needed; the real church, by individuals who are organized by living in Christ—they rejoice in unity beyond space and time. Belonging to a church community or an institutional church does not necessarily make a person part of the real church: "Not everyone who says to me, 'Lord, Lord,' will enter the kingdom of heaven" (Matt 7:21), said Christ. Also, a person called by Christ may or may not belong to a church community or an institutional church—only Christ knows his own.

42. Christ Jesus often prayed alone. That Christ is present among those who gather in his Name does not exclude the need for dedicated solitary practice.

43. There is communion between the visible and the invisible; the invisible is greater and more powerful than the visible, but it works *with* and *within* the visible and is not removed from it.

The real church is the unknown church—a church that often manifests itself through unannounced, unexpected Christians who function within and without church communities, within and without institutional churches; truly, their being and identity defy denominational categorizations. These Christians are known to Christ, while they are at times revealed to each other in the Light of Christ—in an encounter involving the mutual recognition of their divinity. The sum of their actions is the action of the Plan of Christ in the world through the called; but the Plan of Christ is unknown to them, thus unknown to the world.

Truth

The real church is the unbreakable church—it is neither a temple made of stone subject to destruction and decay nor an institution subject to corruption and scandal. The real church is invisible, except to the soul; it is "here" and also "beyond." It operates in the temporal, yet lies in the eternal. Likewise, a Christian aligned with the real church lives (and *is*) in the world while communing with a reality beyond it, and attends to temporal affairs but rests on Eternity. Ultimately, what we call a "Christian" (both as *being* and as *identity*) is a *mystery in Christ*: we find its meaning in the mystical knowledge of the Christ, who is the all-abiding I AM (*being*), as he is the temple of the Living Spirit (*identity*); for "the temple he had spoken of was his body."

CHAPTER 4

Let the Dead Bury Their Own Dead
On Freedom from Family Constructs

1. The Call Is to Go Straight

JESUS SAID, "FOXES HAVE dens and birds have nests, but the Son of Man has no place to lay his head" (Matt 8:20). Even so, he said further, "Follow me, and let the dead bury their own dead" (8:22).[1]

To follow Christ means (always) to follow him to a placeless land. Christ speaks to the heart, calling us to live a New Way which does not resemble the old. Christ says, "No one who puts a hand to the plow and looks back is fit for service in the kingdom of God" (Luke 9:62). That is, no one who looks back can go straight—following his Way.[2] If we look ahead, we will still experience some diversions due to the stones that we encounter as we "plow"; these are the challenges of the Way, but we will persevere. Those who follow Christ shall not look around for idle places: if there is no place to rest for the Son of Man, likewise for those who follow him; we are to find joy in the work we do in the world while being conscious of the Light that testifies of the emerging kingdom. As Christ said: "Let the dead

---

1. See also Luke 9:58, 60. These two sayings appear together in the Gospels. They are often addressed as *the cost of following Jesus*.

2. Ananias, a disciple, is told by Christ in a vision to go to the street called Straight to restore the sight of Paul. He does so, giving the Holy Spirit to Paul, who is subsequently baptized (Acts 9:10–19). This passage may be seen as a metaphor here. On *straight paths* for the LORD, see Isa 40:3; Matt 3:3; Mark 1:3; Luke 3:4; John 1:23; Acts 13:10 ESV.

bury their own dead, but you go and proclaim the kingdom of God" (Luke 9:60). It is like learning to ride a bicycle: you must look ahead—not back, not sideways, but to what lies in front of you—so that when you face a stone you may prevail and not fall to the ground.

2. Negotiation

Jesus said, "Foxes have dens and birds have nests, but the Son of Man has no place to lay his head." Even so, he said further, "Follow me, and let the dead bury their own dead."

We do not listen to Christ carefully.[3] We know that if we do, we will follow him in a straight line. Instead, we look around for alternatives, trying to negotiate the conditions for following him. Christ's burden may be "light" (Matt 11:30), but ours is heavy, as it is familiar—we feel the need to keep our burden for some time so that the people we know may recognize us. Christ said in a parable, "He sent his servant to tell those who had been invited, 'Come, for everything is now ready.' But they all alike began to make excuses" (Luke 14:17–18).[4] That is, we receive God's invitation and go to his house, but just before the "banquet" starts, when the servant calls us to follow him, we say: "I have urgent work to do" or "My family is waiting."[5] Yet, enjoying the banquet of God requires trust without negotiation. Jesus warns in advance those eager to become his disciples: "Foxes have dens and birds have nests, but the Son of Man has no place to lay his head"; that is, in the path of discipleship, conditions are unknown. Even so, life takes care of itself—as it is for the birds and flowers, so it is for those who follow his Way.[6]

Christ gave two major teachings so that those who are called to follow his Way do not fall into making excuses. These teachings represent two levels of Initiation for the called by Christ.

The First Initiation is this: a person called by Christ says, "Lord, first let me go and bury my father" (Luke 9:59). Christ replies, "Let the dead bury their own dead, but you go and proclaim the kingdom of God" (9:60).

---

3. Christ states: "Therefore consider carefully how you listen" (Luke 8:17–18).

4. See the entire parable of the great banquet in Luke 14:15–24.

5. The excuses given in the parable are the demands of personal business and married life (Luke 14:18–20). After this parable, further sayings on discipleship follow (Luke 14:25–35).

6. Matt 6:25–34; Luke 12:22–34; 10:38–42.

That is: those who are called may still wish to fulfill their family duties—those given by commandments such as "Honor your father and mother" (Matt 19:19) and those agreed upon by society—but Christ wants us to look ahead and do what is required for the kingdom of God to become a living reality. This is the priority. Christ does not deny the importance of family duties; for he did *not* say, "Let the dead bury their own dead, but you rest" or "Let the dead bury their own dead, because burying your father should be irrelevant to you." No; Christ did *not* say such things. You can only leave customs or societal obligations behind when you embrace divine work *actively*. It is God who takes such responsibilities away from you; otherwise, we are to attend to the usual duties—to keep the commandments so as to enter life.[7]

The Second Initiation is this: a person called by Christ says, "I will follow you, Lord; but first let me go back and say goodbye to my family" (Luke 9:61). Christ replies, "No one who puts a hand to the plow and looks back is fit for service in the kingdom of God" (9:62). This is a harder saying, for those who remain will worry about the departure of those they love. Even so, when the call comes, we are not to look back at first; Jesus knows that if we take the time to say goodbye, our family will try to convince us not to follow him, and we will start making excuses (like in the parable). Consequently, we must trust that we will again see those we love—our families (as also our dead)—in going forward, following the Way. (These are the two levels of Initiation given by Christ so that we do not make excuses.)

In our times, Christ's call to follow him without burying our father or saying goodbye to our family may seem inapplicable; but this is so only as long as we imagine it incorrectly. That is, Christians still want to know what to do, not how to be. But the call of Christ is always existential—never a rule that can be easily followed. Christ's urgency implies his trust in Eternity, *as if* he were saying: "Come now; there is no 'goodbye,' for there is Eternity, but the work for the light kingdom is urgent." Certainly, Jesus did *not* tell his disciples to avoid their families—Jesus himself maintained contact with his family,[8] and his disciples may have done likewise.[9] Working

---

7. "If you want to enter life, keep the commandments" (Matt 19:17).

8. See John 2:12, for example.

9. From Jesus' reply to Peter in Luke 18:28–30, we may assume that the disciples had left "home or wife or brothers or sisters or parents or children for the sake of the kingdom of God" (18:29), at least during the three years of Jesus' ministry. Even so, they may have made occasional visits; for example, Jesus visited the house of Peter and Andrew (with both of them together with James and John) and healed Peter's mother-in-law (Matt

for the kingdom is not an enterprise separate from family and society; but Christ's call breaks through group-isolation tendencies, including those supported by societal customs and family duties. It thus asks the Christian to embrace the possibility of universal brotherhood in a broader society based on Love. As Christians, we are to follow Christ's call without negotiation.

3. Worry and Spiritual Family

Jesus said, "Foxes have dens and birds have nests, but the Son of Man has no place to lay his head." Even so, he said further, "Follow me, and let the dead bury their own dead."

The earthly family[10] is always worrying. It is a well-minded worry, however, for the earthly family is "always there" when everything falls apart. Yet, the service of the kingdom—the commitment to truth—is generally far from its reach. In the Gospels, the nature of Jesus' relationship with his earthly family is not clear. Nevertheless, we know that the family of Jesus worried about him. Jesus' mother—Mary—understood his mission, yet she worried and suffered as a mother.[11] Jesus' kin also worried, in their case without sympathy toward his mission, for they did not understand him.[12] Certainly, the feeling of proximity to a prophet does not favor the

---

8:14–15; Mark 1:29–31). Little is known regarding the contact kept by the disciples with their families (see 1 Cor 9:5). Nowadays, communication technologies make it almost inconceivable not to be able to keep any contact with families, even for missionaries working in relatively isolated places.

10. The earthly family includes blood relatives; those who, not being the biological parents, have exercised the function of parents; adopted children; those caring for and cared for; close childhood friends and friends from youth; those linked through an affectionate worldly relationship. In contrast, the spiritual family encompasses all those with whom one has spiritual bonds, constituting a communion based on brotherhood, sisterhood, and friendship in God. Earthly family members can be part of the spiritual family.

11. The wedding at Cana in Galilee (John 2:1–12) was the first time Jesus "revealed his glory" (2:11), and it happened because of Mary's encouragement. But Mary also suffered greatly as a mother: "A sword will pierce your own soul" (Luke 2:35), said Simeon to her at the temple.

12. "For even his own brothers did not believe in him" (John 7:5); see also Mark 3:20–21. Most Christian denominations hold that Jesus did not have carnal brothers or sisters; that is, the word "brothers" in the Gospels would mean another type of relative, or someone pertaining to the family circle or the closer community. See the Greek term *adelphos*, meaning "*a brother, near kinsman or relative; one of the same nation or nature; one of equal rank and dignity; an associate, a member of the Christian community*"

understanding of their mission. Jesus' hometown is known to be the worst context for his work—he healed a few, but many questioned his authority and teaching only because they knew his family (i.e., they felt too close to him). Thus, Jesus said, "A prophet is not without honor except in his own town, among his relatives and in his own home" (Mark 6:4).[13] Just as parents hardly understand their sons and daughters, and yet they care and worry about them, any member of the earthly family may care and worry, still rarely understanding someone's spiritual journey as others do.[14]

It had to be through family worries—through the exposure of the fears of the earthly family in regard to a prophet's mission—that Christ Jesus gave his central teaching on the spiritual family. It happens in a crowded house while maintaining a harsh dialogue with the Pharisees and the teachers of the law. The Pharisees have already begun plotting how to kill Jesus after his challenge to the strict observance of the Sabbath (the tipping point of many confrontations).[15] Now, they are accusing him of healing a demon-possessed man as an agent of the prince of demons.[16] Rumors spread fast, and Jesus' family comes in a hurry. As Jesus is dismantling the accusations, someone approaches him and tells him that his mother and brothers are waiting outside, desiring to speak to him. Christ's reply is unexpected: "Who is my mother, and who are my brothers?" (Matt 12:48). Then, pointing to his disciples, he says: "Here are my mother and my brothers. For whoever does the will of my Father in heaven is my brother and sister and mother" (12:49–50).[17] Such is the spiritual family according to Christ: *those who do the will of the Father.*

This saying of Christ is hard for Christians, because they immediately think about the worry of Jesus' mother and brothers, who seem to have been ignored by Jesus. But this saying is not about Jesus' mother and brothers—it is about the service of the kingdom and the commitment to truth. The person who interrupts Jesus to tell him that his family is looking for him

---

(Mounce, *Interlinear New Testament*, 1002). A *hermeneutics of freedom* would emphasize Jesus' perspective on the spiritual family first and foremost; also, Jesus' entrusting of John to his mother (as her own son) and of his mother to John (as his own mother), points toward a further understanding of this subject (John 19:25–27).

13. See entire passage in Mark 6:1–6; also Matt 13:53–58; Luke 4:14–29; John 4:44; 6:41–42.

14. Earthly relatives who see beyond the flesh are rare.

15. Matt 12:1–14.

16. Matt 12:22–37.

17. See the entire passage in Matt 12:46–50.

represents those who put the earthly family above everything else—family worries over divine work, in this case. Jesus' reply challenges those who consider the worries of kin above the service of the kingdom. Furthermore, Jesus calls his listeners to acknowledge the spiritual family—the family that is "not of the world" (John 17:14, 16).[18] Hence, the ancestral family worries are confronted by Jesus through his uncompromising surrender to the task at hand; at the same time, he introduces the idea of a family *in* God—the understanding of the family as not determined by blood or worldly bonds of any kind. Christ's saying, "Who is my mother, and who are my brothers?" is not a critique of his worrying earthly family (Jesus is not speaking to his beloved mother and his brothers waiting at the door). His words are directed to those who think that earthly family worries are important enough to stop the work that needs to be done or to silence the words that need to be said for the coming of the kingdom of the Living God.

4. Rejection of Inheritance

Jesus said, "Foxes have dens and birds have nests, but the Son of Man has no place to lay his head." Even so, he said further, "Follow me, and let the dead bury their own dead."

Christ gave strong warnings to prevent family relationships from hindering the New Way he was opening. To the disciples, he said: "Anyone who loves their father or mother more than me is not worthy of me; anyone who loves their son or daughter more than me is not worthy of me" (Matt 10:37–38). This saying is not as hard as it seems. For Christ did *not* say that his disciples should love their father, mother, sons, and daughters *less* than before; he said that they ought to love him—the Light and the Life—more than them. It is our lack of understanding of Divine Love—our presumption that love is limited—that makes us think that the love for Christ must come at the expense of loving our family. This premise is false. The love for Christ must be above any love, because it does not limit any other love but enhances it: it amplifies and harmonizes any love with the Divine Love immanent in creation. Thus, by loving Christ more than anybody else, Christians shall love their families (and anybody else) *more*—not less!

Christ gave another saying as a condition for becoming a disciple. When crowds were following him, he turned and said: "If anyone comes

---

18. Jesus' disciples, who are his spiritual "mother," "sisters," and "brothers" (Matt 12:49–50), are "not of the world" (John 17:14, 16).

to me and does not hate father and mother, wife and children, brothers and sisters—yes, even their own life—such a person cannot be my disciple" (Luke 14:25–26).[19] Such a statement, at first, means the obvious—that no earthly family relationship should get in the way of discipleship, just as no other attachment should do so; for Jesus continued saying: "Those of you who do not give up everything you have cannot be my disciples" (14:33).[20] Yet further, this saying has another meaning as *experienced* once one has entered the actual path of discipleship: "hate"[21] does not mean that we should feel animosity toward our families but that we ought to *reject* the traumas or shadows of heredity—the family inheritance that keeps us bound—so that we may grow into the Light of a regenerated new creation.[22] It is the ancestral meaning of the various types of relationships that we must reject, not the persons. Thus: by rejecting the ancestral meaning of "father," "mother," and "children," we free the burden passed through generations; by rejecting the ancestral meaning of "husband" and "wife," we free ourselves from the inherited patterns of sexism and oppression in marital

---

19. In following Christ, one is to renounce *ordinary** earthly family relationships; however, the use of "hate" here is not clear and needs an explanation. That is, first, to his disciples, Christ gave a milder saying—is one first to hate their family (in order to become a disciple) and then, as disciple, to love Christ more than their previously repudiated family? It does not make sense. Second, Christ said that you should honor your father and your mother to enter life, and that you should love your enemies—are Christians meant to both hate and honor their parents at the same time, or hate their families and love their enemies? No. It cannot be. (*The renunciation of *ordinariness* does *not* mean plainly renouncing earthly family relationships.)

20. Jesus' tone is severe; he needs to convey to the multitudes the difficulty of his new path.

21. In Luke 14:26, most English Bibles use the word "hate." However, comparing this passage with others in the New Testament, we see that "hate" could be also understood as "reject"; that is, "hate" does not mean an emotion toward something but instead an existential reaction of rejection; for example: "Everyone who does evil hates [rejects] the light, and will not come into the light for fear that their deeds will be exposed" (John 3:20); "If the world hates [rejects] you, keep in mind that it hated [rejected] me first" (John 15:18). An examination of a variety of Bible translations, including translations in other languages (e.g., Spanish), shows many other alternatives; hence, there is doubt and debate on how this saying should be translated and interpreted.

22. A person who has not rejected the family inheritance is not free from its ways: "'If you were Abraham's children,' said Jesus, 'then you would do what Abraham did. As it is, you are looking for a way to kill me, a man who has told you the truth that I heard from God. *Abraham did not do such things*. You are doing *the works of your own father*'" (John 8:39–41, emphasis added).

relations;[23] by rejecting the ancestral meaning of "brothers" and "sisters," we abhor Cain-like tendencies, establishing an eternal friendship in Christ.[24] We are not to reject our inheritance without Christ but *in* Christ; because Christ is the Light that frees our being, even to its physical degree, from the burdens of inheritance. Christ said: "So if the Son sets you free, you will be free indeed" (John 8:36).[25]

The burdens of inheritance are both physical and psychological. Harmful physical inheritance must be freed so that the body is brought to transformation into the Light of Christ. Christ's Resurrection points to a different way of relating to the body. We are not to reject the body, nor the positive aspects of inheritance that contribute to its formation and development; yet, the misalignments and traumas inherited throughout generations need to be freed, as they prevent us from being the Light that we are in an *embodied* manner. Harmful psychological inheritances must be freed as well. Jesus gave a teaching to the disciples addressing precisely such an inheritance: that of the father molding the son, the mother molding the daughter, and the mother-in-law molding the daughter-in-law. Christ Jesus states: "Do not suppose that I have come to bring peace to the earth. I did not come to bring peace, but a sword. For I have come to turn 'a man against his father, a daughter against her mother, a daughter-in-law against her mother-in-law—a man's enemies will be the members of his own household'" (Matt 10:34–36).[26] Indeed, when our father, mother, or mother-in-law try to mold us, they may appear to be "enemies," just as Christ said. But following Christ involves *refusing to be molded* by our father, mother, or mother-in-law; we are to especially reject any psychological inheritance which does not honor our freedom *in* Christ. Only then we can be free; only then may we have a healthy relationship with our earthly family and, consequently, love our family *more*. Christ brings a sword

---

23. One of the ways to reject the family inheritance is through holy matrimony—the female and male principles of the cosmos unite to create a spiritual whole, a new family not bound by ties of blood (see Matt 19:4–6; Gen 2:24). Yet, marriage is rarely understood in this manner; it has become a sociocultural act—a custom rather than a holy mystery.

24. All the degenerative habits inherited from the earthly family need to be rejected, including those acquired through friendships. Among friendships, those of youth are particularly linked to behavioral patterns; if negative, they are to be freed. For example, judgmental cruelty, physical and psychological bulling, and sexism are tendencies developed during this early period of life; we need to be liberated by *rejecting* ("hating") the types of relationships and group dynamics which favored them.

25. See John 8:31–41 (entire passage).

26. See also Mic 7:6.

which cuts the bounding strings of heredity. It is not a physical sword but the "double-edged sword" (Rev 1:16) of the Word, which makes us free.

5. Universal Family

Jesus said, "Foxes have dens and birds have nests, but the Son of Man has no place to lay his head." Even so, he said further, "Follow me, and let the dead bury their own dead."

Christ's position on the family is based on eternal being. What an "ideal family" may be—according to societal customs, economic needs, or biological functions—seems irrelevant to the Son of God. However, even if Christ's position does not lead to the advocacy of conventional family views, he does not discard family relationships either. Further (and of relevance to contemporary thought), Christ's sayings concerning the family—loving him more, rejecting the shadows of heredity, not saying goodbye when following him—question family constructs, yet they are not "deconstructive" in the sense that we understand deconstruction today. That is, Christ's teachings are *not a postmodern critique* of traditional family constructs but rather an eternal critique to any family construct that is not based on communion and Love. The Way of Christ works upon wholeness, and there is something in common with well-done deconstruction in that sense,[27] but the wholeness of Christ means regeneration into Life and freedom—it comes through spiritual means and divine assertion, not as a result of philosophical inquiry and skillful discourse.[28]

There is not a single family model that guarantees (and represents) an ideal life shared with others; healthy family models are never fixed, for they maintain a dialogue with life. Thus, there is no particular family model that we should keep in mind and try to follow; it results only in unhappiness, just

27. Well-done deconstruction often presumes a wholeness, and that such wholeness is not obvious. It works especially well with paradigms constructed on opposites, where one side is traditionally weaker or less favored. Deconstruction seeks to problematize constructs that are taken for granted, ideas that create division and often injustice.

28. Christ came to fulfill: "Do not think that I have come to abolish the Law or the Prophets; I have not come to abolish them but to fulfill them" (Matt 5:17); "Out of his fullness we have all received grace in place of grace already given" (John 1:16). At the same time, there will be those who embrace Christ's New Way and those who will follow the old ways, for they cannot handle the new: "And no one pours new wine into old wineskins. Otherwise, the new wine will burst the skins; the wine will run out and the wineskins will be ruined. No, new wine must be poured into new wineskins. And no one after drinking old wine wants the new, for they say, 'The old is better'" (Luke 5:37–39).

like the pursuit of a goal that can never be attained. Besides, the idealization of a particular family model excludes and degrades other possible and necessary alternatives, generating pernicious, unwanted effects. Just as the idealization of the traditional family is perverse in its insensitivity to those who have been abandoned, conceived in rape, abused by their parents, or have lost their parents in their youth, any idealized model can have pernicious effects. A Christianity which honors Christ's Way is a Christianity that is flexible and embodies Christ's teaching of a *universal family in God*. Thus, "father" is anyone who takes the task of true and loving fatherhood, and "mother" is anyone who takes the task of true and loving motherhood; these are our venerable father and mother; they can be our "natural" parents but also our grandparents, stepparents, an aunt or an uncle, a friend, or any person whatsoever who ever took on such responsibility with love and generosity. These are the true parents to be honored, as the commandment "honor your father and mother" says (Matt 19:19).[29]

It is the way we exist that determines the realization of our Christian venture, not society's approval of our enterprise. It is the internal beauty of our lives that matters, not external appearances and ephemeral success. Life and not fixed dogmas, faith and not immovable beliefs, are what form the basis of the Christian Way. Thus: "family," for a Christian, means *family in Christ*—divine relationships beyond bonds of kin and law. It does not exclude members of the earthly family, but it is always beyond the ties of kinship and the ways of the world. Within such an understanding of the family, the different types of relationships are circumstantial. Certainly, with Christ we can have different relationships: as sons and daughters of God, we are also brothers and sisters[30] of Christ; as disciples of Christ, we may also reach fellowship and communion with him and the Father;[31] and Christ, being one with the Father, can be fatherlike[32] at times as well. All these relationships are possible with Christ, even if Christ, primordially, as the Light of being, is known as our truest "I" and luminous self. In sum: because with Christ—the Logos and Life—there is not a single fixed way of relating, we shall not impose fixed ways of relating and thus family models

---

29. Wholeness in Christ requires thinking in a creative way through the Spirit that came in his Name, honoring his Way and his empathy as well.

30. Heb 2:11; Rom 8:29.

31. John 15:15; 1 John 1:3; Heb 3:14.

32. Not an unusual position for patristic writers; see Palamas, *Triads*, 67, 136n80, 133n38.

6. Beyond Childhood and Parenthood

Jesus said, "Foxes have dens and birds have nests, but the Son of Man has no place to lay his head." Even so, he said further, "Follow me, and let the dead bury their own dead."

To follow Christ implies letting go of childhood and parenthood—to become adults in Christ. In realizing and embodying Christ's Being, parents shall come to see their grown-up sons and daughters as brothers, sisters, and friends; likewise, sons and daughters shall see their parents as brothers, sisters, and friends. If we follow Christ without looking back to the family roles once held, we will see how our family relationships develop into spiritual relationships that nurture mutual growth. The extent to which such a change in family relationships is realized represents the degree of our transformation as society in Christ, for in Christ there are no fathers and sons, or mothers and daughters—we are all "born of God" (John 1:12–13). There will be those who resist; fearful of the change, they will call us from behind. Our call is to look forward and say: "Come and face me while I walk; then, walk with me as my brother, sister, and friend; for there is much work to do and many mysteries of the light kingdom to be revealed; we shall enjoy them together in the path that lies ahead."

Misunderstood parenthood is a major limitation for the actualization of the light kingdom in society; it reflects the desires of parental mentors to retain their roles so as to experience everlasting parenthood within hereditary continuity. Parental mentors need to inspect their desires in light of the Christian understanding of life. When they think, "My sons and daughters will always be children for me," they should remember that children are gifts of Life to life (embodiment) and from life to Life (spiritual growth), and are not to remain as "children," even figuratively. And when they think, "I know my sons and daughters better than they know themselves; they need my guidance, otherwise they are lost," they should remember that Divine Light is the "substance" in which the eternal soul is birthed,[33] and that God is the true guide of our lives.[34] Who we are (and are to become) no person can know, for in the Light of being, we are a mystery even to

---

33. Matt 5:14–16.
34. Job 29:3; Ps 18:28; John 12:46.

ourselves. Parental mentors do not realize the harm that such attitudes can cause; hence, they make it difficult for their sons and daughters to grow up as adults in God. In contrast to the desire of everlasting parenthood within hereditary continuity, Christ demands the *welcoming of discontinuity*, with conflict if necessary—son against father, daughter against mother[35]—unless the letting go of childhood and parenthood occurs.

Therefore, children and their parental mentors are to become brothers, sisters, and friends in God; such is Christian adulthood. Once Christian adulthood is reached, those who exercised the function of parental mentors shall be able to learn *with* their sons and daughters (now brothers, sisters, and friends) and also *from* them. Likewise, those who were sons and daughters shall be able to learn *with* their parental mentors (now brothers, sisters, and friends), not only *from* them and *in spite of* them. Both parental mentors and their sons and daughters shall accept the mystery of God within each other and also that, notwithstanding the years lived together (and their genuine mutual affection), they have *never known each other so well*. Further, they shall realize that they are to be friends in a greater brotherhood beyond earthly family bonds and boundaries, which engulfs them and sets them free—independent—as adults in God.

7. No Home but God

Jesus said, "Foxes have dens and birds have nests, but the Son of Man has no place to lay his head." Even so, he said further, "Follow me, and let the dead bury their own dead."

Attachment to the earthly family is often connected to a physical place—the family home. To "come back home" often means reencountering the traditions and customs we were raised with. Christ Jesus warned those who intended to follow him that his Way transcends both the family home and society's traditions and customs. When a teacher of the law said to him, "I will follow you wherever you go" (Matt 8:19), he replied: "Foxes have dens and birds have nests, but the Son of Man has no place to lay his head" (8:20). That is, Christ's Way transcends any physical home. Further, when a disciple said to him, "Let me go and bury my father" (Matt 8:21), he replied: "Follow me, and let the dead bury their own dead" (8:22). Thus, Christ's Way also transcends society's traditions and customs. Such are the implications of following Christ through a continuous commitment. The

---

35. Matt 10:34–36. See section 4.

Christian Way is this: no home but God; no tradition or custom but working for the light kingdom *actively*.[36]

Thus, following Christ implies constantly working for the kingdom—for the manifestation of the immanent Light in creation—without attachment to any home. Then Christ and the Father will make a home with us. As Jesus said: "Anyone who loves me will obey my teaching. My Father will love them, and we will come to them and make our home with them" (John 14:23).[37] The promise is thus of a permanent home with Christ and the Father, regardless of where we are. Such a promise unburdens our being from the need of finding rest in a particular physical home, prompting the acknowledgement of the Divine as all-pervading, which provides a permanent existential home. In sum: we are not to depend on a physical home; yet, we can find our true home—one made by the Father and Son—in a conscious and constant manner.

As we make ourselves fitted for the Father and Son to make their home with us, we shall also contribute to making the New Earth[38] a living reality. That is, we should seek to improve the conditions of the Earth so that it becomes fitted for the Father and Son to make their home in it as well. In doing so, we align our works with those of the One who says: "I am making everything new!" (Rev 21:5). Living in a New Earth implies a different way of apprehending reality but also of engaging with reality. The work to be done demands that we find love in our labor, discipline in our surrender, and sacrifice in our humility. To work in this way is easier if we find a spiritual family—spiritual companions who are dispassionate in regard to society's traditions and customs (they will provide support as we cocreate new conditions to live in). We shall work toward the betterment of our life conditions until we are able to say: "We were dead, but now we are alive; we were lost, but now we are found;[39] for we are finally in the boundless home made by the Father and Son."

---

36. The parable of the bags of gold (Matt 25:14–30) portrays how those who serve the LORD must work for the kingdom *actively*. See also Rom 12:11.

37. Most Bible translations (NIV, ESV, etc.) use "home" for the Greek term *monē/n* ("*a stay in any place; an abode, dwelling, mansion*, Jn. 14:2, 23" [Mounce, *Interlinear New Testament*, 1116]). The "home" made by the Father and Son is further completed by the Spirit (John 16:7), understood as "Helper" (ESV, NKJV) or "Advocate" (NIV).

38. Rev 21:1.

39. The passage of the parable of the prodigal son, echoed here, reads: "But we had to celebrate and be glad, because this brother of yours was dead and is alive again; he was lost and is found" (Luke 15:32).

Truth

Christianity best presents itself when not trying to find its place in the world—it is the world which must find its place and adapt to the boundless Light of the coming kingdom. For Christ's kingdom is not of this world (in Jesus' time and today).[40] Because the Christian impulse is to embrace all existence, any attempt to find safety in a particular place, tradition, or custom (i.e., to find safety in the world) diverts our attention from the Heart of reality we are called to live. Christ's call is to a path depending neither on location (for "the Son of Man has no place to lay his head") nor on traditions or customs (for "the dead" are to "bury their own dead"). The Heart of reality is found everywhere, regardless of the place and the society in which we appear to be.

---

40. During his ministry, Christ Jesus rejected being made king: "Jesus, knowing that they intended to come and make him king by force, withdrew again to a mountain by himself" (John 6:15). Christ said to Pilate: "My kingdom is not of this world. If it were, my servants would fight to prevent my arrest by the Jewish leaders. But now my kingdom is from another place" (John 18:36).

CHAPTER 5

Will Set You Free
Truth Explorations and Openings of Being

1. The Proof of Truth

CHRISTIANITY IS A PATH to freedom (it should be); hence, Christian existence should manifest freedom—the freedom of being. Jesus said to those who believed in him: "If you hold to my teaching, you are really my disciples. Then you will know the truth, and the truth will set you free" (John 8:31–32). Consequently, Christian practice should lead to the experience of freedom. A freedom that is revealed by Christ, as Jesus also assured: "So if the Son sets you free, you will be free indeed" (John 8:36).[1]

Yet, to present Christianity as a path to freedom is difficult today: oppression and censorship have been part of Christian history—exercised by Christians themselves. We must thus rediscover the foundations of Christ's Way. In doing so, freedom becomes a central experience for the Christian. To that end, the Christianity of today should be the following: first, calm and peaceful, far from the violence exercised in the past; second, humble—thoroughly unassuming—in its dialogue with the many faith traditions

---

1. The hermeneutical reading of these sayings is broad here—the Son frees from sin but also presents a teaching that brings freedom. These themes are explored throughout this chapter.

and philosophies of the world;[2] third, graceful and not condemnatory.[3] A Christianity relevant today must be *a Christianity of freedom*,[4] for the Son is the truth, and his teaching leads to the truth,[5] but the proof of it lies in our freedom.

2. Disciples and Freedom

Jesus said, "You will know the truth, and the truth will set you free."

Being a Christian does not inevitably make a person a disciple of Christ. To be a Christian, one must believe in Christ. To be a disciple of Christ, one must follow Christ's teaching. Hence, a person can be a Christian (a believer) but not a disciple. It follows the words of Christ. He said to those who *already believed*: "If you hold to my teaching, you are really my disciples" (John 8:31).[6] And so: there are those who believe and do not follow Christ's teaching; in order to truly be a disciple, one needs to hold to Christ's teaching (in his time and today). Further, Christ continued saying that by holding to his teaching they would know the truth, and that would make them free. The sequence of Initiation is thus clear: belief in Christ begets holding to his teaching (through commitment in discipleship); holding to his teaching begets truth (through practice); truth begets freedom (through transformation). If a Christian does not experience freedom—the liberating experience of truth—it is because there is no real

---

2. There is a Catholic tradition of interreligious/interfaith dialogue that has moved in this direction, especially after Vatican II. This tradition includes individuals such as Thomas Merton, Raimon Panikkar, Henri Le Saux, Bede Griffiths, Thomas Keating, David Steindl-Rast, Francis X. Clooney, and Mario I. Aguilar, among others. Their approaches vary—some more experiential, others more academic—but fairness to the religious "other" and transformative learning are of crucial importance for all of them. See, for example, Panikkar, *Intrareligious Dialogue*; Clooney, *Learning Interreligiously*; Aguilar, *Way of the Hermit*; Steindl-Rast, *i am*, 90–113.

3. The three chosen characteristics are supported by Scripture. See, for example, John 14:27; 16:33; 20:19, 21, 26; Matt 8:26; Mark 4:39; Matt 11:29–30; John 3:17.

4. "Now the Lord is the Spirit, and where the Spirit of the Lord is, there is freedom" (2 Cor 3:17).

5. The Son is the truth (*alētheia*) (John 14:6); his teachings lead us to know the truth (*alētheia/n*) (John 8:32).

6. See John 8:30–32. See also Luke 6:46–49, where Jesus explains that those who hear his sayings and put them "into practice" (6:47) lay their "foundation on rock" (6:48), while those who do not, end up "without foundation" (6:49).

consideration of the teaching of Christ (i.e., no commitment or practice), and so no transformation through discipleship.

Consequently, while faith and sincere belief are necessary for discipleship, they are not enough: Christ's teachings are to be consciously practiced and experienced. For this reason, in becoming a disciple, one should differentiate between the domains of faith and belief, and practice and experience. For example: faith is in Christ, but his teachings on forgiveness are to be practiced and experienced; and belief is in Christ's Resurrection, but Christ's teachings on seeing God are to be practiced and experienced. Hence, a disciple has faith in Christ and believes in the Resurrection just as any other Christian, but also practices forgiveness in prayer and deeds and engages in contemplation and inquiry to cultivate the experience of God. In sum: a disciple employs all means necessary to make Christ's teachings alive within their own being and consciousness; for faith and belief are not enough if we are to follow Christ's very Word.

Jesus said that those who hold to his teaching will know the truth. He also prayed for the experience of truth to be stabilized in the consciousness of his disciples; he asked the Father: "Sanctify them in the truth; your word is truth" (John 17:17 ESV). One can be *sanctified in* the "truth" because truth is an experience—it is the confirmation of the Christian faith; but such an experience is not automatic. This is the reason why Christ Jesus prayed for those who were his *disciples already* (those truly committed to practicing the Way) to be sanctified in the truth—to come to true freedom. Hence, we should remember: to become a Christian, either at birth or during one's lifetime, is not enough to experience the freedom given by Christ and his teaching.[7] Such is a fact we shall be ready to accept, for Christians do not experience freedom just by calling themselves "Christians" (i.e., by simply believing and experiencing an initial relief).[8] On the contrary, some Christians seem far from freedom, as they are far from truth. Christians tend to forget that an *entire work* needs to be done in order to experience and embody the freedom given by Christ—to become "a Christian" was *never enough to be free*. Thus, Christians must earn their freedom by holding to the teachings of Christ; otherwise, they are to remain in a state of comforting belief.

---

7. See, again, John 8:31–32.

8. Relief and other initial liberating experiences upon accepting the faith are not the same as freedom.

3. The Threefold Teaching of Freedom

Jesus said, "You will know the truth, and the truth will set you free."

A teaching that offers true freedom must deal with all dimensions of human life. Experiencing freedom in our individual spiritual practice is not enough—all life's interactions must be freed. Christ Jesus gave such a teaching in a way comprehensive enough for his time and the circumstances of his ministry. His concern extended to relational, cultural, and systemic issues, as we would categorize them today. Hence, he offered a path that freed our being from relational struggles, cultural constraints, and the structural forces of power, at the same time bestowing the Divine Power and Light which made such liberation possible. Focusing on these dimensions of life, Christ presented a *threefold teaching of freedom* which is the means to the (meant-to-be) broad experience of freedom distinctive to the Christian Way.

Freedom from relational struggles—from the ways we are bound through resentment—was given through Christ's constant call to forgiveness.[9] He also showed how it is possible to transform acts of violence into opportunities for transformation (e.g., by turning the other cheek to those conscious enough to understand their mistaken use of violence,[10] or by challenging those coming with weapons to arrest him while also healing the servant whose ear a follower cut off[11]). Through the practice of these teachings, together with those related to freedom from family burdens,[12] helping and healing others, etc., and always with the awareness of Christ-like Love[13] oriented to self-giving, Christians may recover their autonomy in God in the face of human relations.

---

9. Matt 6:12–15; 18:21–35; Mark 11:25–26; Luke 11:4; 17:3; 23:34 (ultimate forgiveness on the cross).

10. An alternative to "eye for eye"; see Matt 5:38–39; Luke 6:29. There are various interpretations of this saying. Here, I refer to a usual experience for many: turning the other cheek as a spontaneous reaction that generates self-awareness. A *hermeneutics of freedom* would not favor passive-pacifism interpretations (for they advocate fixed behavior regardless of circumstances) or active-nonviolent-resistance interpretations (for they may suggest Jesus' spiritual behavior as being not spontaneous and willed by the Father but as ruled by strategized political action). Christian pacifism comes from existential peace (i.e., the so-called "peace within"), but with a dynamic, spontaneous, and flexible quality that cannot be reduced to fixed rules of conduct.

11. Luke 22:50–52; see also Matt 26:51–55; Mark 14:47–50; John 18:10–11.

12. See chapter 4.

13. See chapter 1.

Freedom from cultural constraints was given through Christ's example to live in service of the truth, as willed by the Father.[14] Serving the truth makes any constraining dogma, social convention, or unfeeling behavior confront their dark side in the sight of divine duty motivated by Love. The Life willed by the Father does not respect religious observances (e.g., the Sabbath,[15] the Sunday) when there is divine work to be done; it does not respect social conventions and traditions (e.g., the elders' tradition of the washing of hands[16] or fasting[17]) when there is relational joy to be expressed; it does not respect unfeeling behavior masked as a righteous deed (e.g., suggesting that the perfume poured on Jesus' head be sold and the proceeds given to the poor[18]). Taking as an example Jesus' reactions, together with his relentless critique of false righteousness (e.g., praying and giving alms in public to be seen by others), Christians can unmask the sense of a Divine Existence not bounded by traditions and cultural constraints.

Freedom from the structural forces of power was given through Christ's call to surrender to divine providence so that one's relationship with the political and economic domains is not strategized and one is not subjected to their ways. One cannot negotiate the stance of one's heart—that is, "serve two masters" (Matt 6:24)[19]—therefore, a Christian is to put all "treasures in heaven" (6:20),[20] accepting that God will provide for them as needed.[21] Christians may be persecuted or tolerated,

---

14. John 3:2; 5:19; 12:49; 14:10, 11, 24.

15. See, for example, Matt 12:1–14; Mark 2:23—3:6; Luke 6:1–11; 13:10–17; 14:1–6; John 5:1–30; 7:21–24; 9:13–34.

16. In Matt 15:1–20 and Mark 7:1–23, the Pharisees are accusing Jesus' disciples of not washing their hands, which breaks with "the tradition of the elders" (7:3, 5); then, Jesus explains how the Pharisees are breaking "the commands of God" (7:8–9) for the sake of their self-serving tradition. (See also Luke 11:37–54, where Jesus is signaled for the same issue, thus triggering the woes on the Pharisees and the experts in the law.)

17. Mark 2:18–19.

18. Such thinking is unfeeling—it does not acknowledge the high devotion and purpose expressed in the act—and so it becomes the object of Jesus' critique. Further, the pouring of perfume can be understood as a preparation for what is to come—the Passion of Christ. See Matt 26:6–13; Mark 14:1–11; John 12:1–8. In John, the woman is identified as Mary, the perfume is poured on Jesus' feet, and Judas Iscariot is identified as the disciple criticizing the act. (Luke 7:36–50 seems to describe a different event.)

19. See also Luke 16:13.

20. Matt 6:19–24; Luke 12:33–34. See also Luke 18:22 or Luke 12:13–21.

21. Matt 6:25–34; Luke 12:22–31. A *hermeneutics of freedom* would not defend a literal reading; that is, to be provided for at times means to have one's own resources as well.

depending on the sociopolitical circumstances in which they live. Yet, their alliance shall be all the same—to the Living God; for true freedom is found solely in God. This is what Jesus' saying, "Give back to Caesar what is Caesar's, and to God what is God's" (Matt 22:21), means.[22] Through Christ's teachings, we realize that the political and economic domains are not over the divine domain. Thus, we can free ourselves from the power of structural forces—from their effect on our way of thinking—by taking an unnegotiable stance in serving one master: God.

Christ's teachings regarding the relational, cultural, and systemic dimensions of life are not apart from the teachings related to the apprehension of God. Sayings such as "You are the light of the world" (Matt 5:14), "The kingdom of God is in your midst" (Luke 17:21),[23] and "The pure in heart . . . will see God" (Matt 5:8) are realized in the service of the truth and the kingdom while living in the world. From this perspective, the *threefold teaching of freedom* helps the Christian in the understanding of how the perception of God should inform and be in dialogue with one's life. For one may perceive God and yet keep old habits (e.g., be little forgiving, culturally bound, or politically biased); or one may forget such habits for a while only to see them return later in the path. Therefore: to perceive God is not enough to experience all the freedom given by Christ; it is necessary to hold to the teachings of Christ so as to know the truth in its interaction with all of life. Surely, even if one is free in perception, being and living must be included in the quest to freedom; that which is in the Absolute must become in the relative, at least if the aim is Divine Life. Through Christ's teaching, our being is thus established in a freedom that transforms the way we look at society's conventions; the kingdom of God is not to come by repeating the old but through a new way of being—in freedom.

4. Truth and Freedom: The Test of Being

Jesus said, "You will know the truth, and the truth will set you free."

---

22. Matt 22:15–22; Mark 12:13–17; Luke 20:20–26. If Jesus had said, "Do not pay," he would have been accused of acting against Caesar's interests. If Jesus had said, "Do pay," he would have been perceived as cooperating with the Roman rule. Both outcomes were favorable to the Pharisees. Jesus' reply is unexpected—he challenges their mode of thinking, leaving them both amazed and silent.

23. See the other translations of this saying; for example, "The kingdom of God is within you" (Luke 17:21 NKJV).

We wrestle with truth, for truth challenges the tales we tell ourselves to justify our faults and remain the *same*. The consequences are similar to Jacob's wrestling with God: we may wrestle, not seem overpowered, then have our hip wrenched.[24] Wrestling with truth leads to defeat, for truth is simply reality—unshakeable, thus undefeatable. The relationship between truth and freedom is unshakeable as well.[25] That is, "Truth"—the Absolute—is prior to any relative condition, prior to any limit, and so prior to the possibility of bondage or lack of freedom. When Truth is realized, one's being is released into unconditioned freedom—the *state of primordial reality*. Hence, the test of knowing the truth (in line with Jesus' words) is the freedom of being: if we experience freedom, there is truth in our path; if we do not experience freedom, then there is no truth (no matter the lies we tell ourselves).

In the times of Jesus, freedom was thought to reside in political and economic autonomy. The Jews hoped that the forthcoming Messiah would make them free from the Romans (i.e., free from any temporal power far from the ways of the Living God).[26] Quite unexpectedly, however, Christ's general critique during his ministry centered not on the Romans but on the Jewish authorities, who, with their hypocrisy, were failing to guide the Jewish people to find their freedom in God. Christ—as Messiah—worked from within: he called honest, humble, and faithful people to the service of God. His teaching was not concerned with temporary freedom—from the Romans or anyone else—but with the freedom of being. Such a freedom

---

24. Gen 32:22–32. Wrestling with God (or God's will) seems possible, but it has consequences; Jacob's limping because of his hip injury after his wrestling with God is a reminder of it.

25. One may wrestle with freedom, as with truth. Wrestling with freedom happens because the freedom which sprouts from truth is often in conflict with doing what one desires, especially at the beginning of the spiritual path. That is, pursuing one's desires does not make one truly free. For example: the pursuit of pleasure (as experienced through sex, sensations, and senses) leads to further craving; the pursuit of means (power, money, and recognition) leads to attachment and higher demands. Thus, when freedom is misallocated and sought after in anything that is not the truth, then real freedom—the freedom of being—becomes inaccessible; one may have an occasional glimpse of freedom, but it is unlivable without a clear stance in the truth.

26. Even so, in John 8, we have an example of how the Jews did not consider themselves "slaves": "We are Abraham's descendants and have never been slaves of anyone. How can you say that we shall be set free?" (8:33). Are the Egyptian-slavery period and the Babylonian captivity overlooked in this assertion? In any case, throughout this passage, Jesus and the Jews appear to be speaking different "languages," resulting in *a fight over signifieds* on what "freedom" is.

could not be lost and would lead to freedom in all domains. And so, Jesus did not work against the Roman legions; instead, he expelled the "legions" of demons and evil forces, like those residing inside the man living in tombs.[27] Because Christ worked for a type of freedom different from political and economic autonomy—everlasting freedom which would be the base for all other forms of freedom—he was never accepted as the Messiah by the Jewish authorities. Nevertheless, Christ left a clear message for future Christians to remember: a society cannot advocate freedom if the individuals who conform to it do not know *what true freedom is* themselves.

Jesus showed that freedom is an experience that can be lived with recognizable effects. Since the beginning, Christians[28] believed in the Way, risking their lives because it was a path to freedom that was real for them. That is, freedom was a fact confirmed in their existence, in their lives, in their eyes when looking at each other. Christianity was thus founded on freedom, and, for a while, it was free from the oppression and fundamentalism that have been part of its later history. The words of Christ, when he uttered them, were alive. Jesus said: "The words I have spoken to you—they are full of the Spirit and life" (John 6:63). Simon Peter, recognizing it, said: "You have the words of eternal life" (6:68). Christ's *living words* created *openings of being*, and that was the way people knew that they were true—their being would become open to a freedom not known before. Thus, the words of Christ—the Word, the Logos—were the experience of freedom itself, of Life truly lived. It is so today as well. The teachings of Christ lead to truth because they make a person free—truly, fundamentally, existentially. Any teaching of Christ understood in a way contrary to freedom cannot represent truthfully the words of Christ. For Christ's promise is clear—his teaching will set you free.

5. Sin and Truth

Jesus said, "You will know the truth, and the truth will set you free."

Sinning involves acting against the Truth of being,[29] for the root of any expression of sin—a wrongful action, thought, or feeling—is the lack

---

27. "'My name is Legion,' he replied, 'for we are many'" (Mark 5:9–10). See also Luke 8:30.

28. The disciples were first called "Christians" in Antioch (Acts 11:26).

29. See how the Greek term *hamartia*, which means "a missing of the mark" ("error" [Mounce, *Interlinear New Testament*, 1007]), in the New Testament is translated as

of recognition of truth, the lack of resonance with it. Thus, persisting in sinning and the rejection of truth are inescapably related. Jesus made clear the link between a worst sin like murder and the lack of truth in one's self: to those who were seeking to kill him, he said that they did not behave like Abraham's descendants but as the sons of the devil, who was "a murderer from the beginning, not holding to the truth, for there is no truth in him" (John 8:44).[30] Christ also said to them that even if they claimed to be children of God, they did "not belong to God" (8:47), for they did not believe in his Son, who was telling them "the truth" (8:45–46). In their unbelief, they were not free but "slave[s] of sin" (John 8:34 NKJV).[31] Hence: *not* holding to the truth and persisting in sinning are ways of the devil; on the other hand, holding to the truth and becoming free from sin are the Way of Christ.[32] Further, to believe that Christ Jesus is the Son of God, whose power frees the human being from its degenerative tendencies, is the foundation of freedom from sin; Jesus said, "if you do not believe that I am he [the Son of the Father], you will indeed die in your sins" (John 8:24, 27–30).

Christ is the door to the Moral Being—the divine presence and power through which a person is "unmoved" by temptation (i.e., unimpressed by it). The descent and stabilization of the Moral Being in our consciousness infuses inner strength, spiritual autonomy, and capacity of discernment; it thus prevents our falling into the suggestions of the devil (the one who does not have truth in him). But we should remember that the Moral Being does not grant freedom from temptation, which Jesus endured as well. It is the freedom from *falling into* temptation that is given (or at least supported to a great extent). Further, the descent of the Moral Being does not represent all the freedom gained through Christ, for freedom from falling into temptation is not the same as the freedom granted by holding to Christ's teaching; the means is not the same either: the soul's freedom from falling into temptation is given to the faithful believer—through the Moral Being—while the existential freedom that comes from knowing the truth is gained through discipleship—by holding to Christ's teaching. And so, freedom from falling into temptation is different from, even if complementary to, the freedom

---

"sin(s)" (e.g., "Take heart, son; your sins are forgiven" [Matt 9:2]).

30. See John 8:31–47.

31. See John 8:33–34, NKJV.

32. Holding to the truth is contrary to the ways of the devil and of those under his influence. Holding to the truth, just like holding to Christ's teachings (which reveal the truth), is of paramount importance in following the Way of Christ.

realized by knowing the truth through the teachings of Christ; one should *not* get confident in the former and neglect the latter, for without holding to the teachings, we become distracted, coming closer to the ways of the devil—the one in whom there is no truth.

Some Christians fall too often into temptations because they have stopped growing—they feel "stuck." Sometimes, they call themselves "sinners," as if they have a chronic condition with which they have become identified. Yet, according to Scripture, no person "who lives" *in* Christ "keeps on sinning," and further: "No one who continues to sin has either seen him or known him" (1 John 3:6).[33] Hence: Christians that continue sinning have not seen Christ, nor truly known him; they do not live *in* Christ either. Christ said it plainly: "Very truly I tell you, everyone who sins is a slave to sin. Now a slave has no permanent place in the family, but a son belongs to it forever. So if the Son sets you free, you will be free indeed" (John 8:34–36). A Christian is therefore meant to be free from sin (i.e., not from temptation, but from sin); this is clear. Consequently, "sinner" is an improper definition of a Christian; we should use "the light of the world" (Matt 5:14) or "the salt of the earth" (5:13), Christ's chosen words to describe those following him, instead.[34] We become truly aware of sin—the implications of it—when we awaken to the truth ourselves while following Christ's teaching. Thus, Christians should focus not on sin but on the teachings of Christ, for they lead to the truth that sets us free.

6. Preaching and Freedom

Jesus said, "You will know the truth, and the truth will set you free."

Our times are not times for simple preaching: we need to understand the gospel better—to see what it says more clearly.[35] Christianity today is consoling, but it lacks insight and inner transformation. There is a genuine concern for social issues—justice, liberation, equality—but the existential freedom of being and so the challenge to the self are neglected. The

---

33. See 1 John 3:1–6.

34. That there is a battle to overcome "darkness" does not mean that darkness, experienced as various forms of temptation, should define our identity. Our true identity is the Light of truth reflected on and through our being.

35. This statement addresses the Christian world—societies already familiarized with the gospel in a general sense; its concern is the future of established Christianity rather than mission projects and the local needs of a more conventional preaching.

freedom of being is gained through the living exploration of the gospel; such an inquiry requires spiritual curiosity, attention to detail, and searching for the experience of God. Christians know the gospel; however, they have forgotten their curiosity, do not pay attention to detail, and highly neglect the experience of God. Understanding the gospel is not to be taken for granted: it is necessary to revisit the gospel as a regular practice—not to confirm our ideas but to discover insights we had not seen before. Likewise, the experience of God is not to be neglected: Christianity started with an experience—that of Jesus receiving the Spirit from above, then the Spirit immediately being given to others through the Baptism of the Spirit Force;[36] many other experiences ensued. And so, the Christian work of today should be to develop an *exploratory Christianity*: a new *praxis of freedom* grounded in the experience of God, the attentive reading of Christ's teachings, and deep spiritual practice while embracing the questions and concerns of contemporary life.

Some Christians may not be able to envision Christianity as based on exploration and inquiry. Many think of preaching their own version of Christianity, often against other versions (it seems to them a matter of asserting a set of beliefs); in doing so, they preach Christianity as if the experience of God, Christ Jesus' words, and the social problems of today are less important than their own ideas and convictions. These approaches bind people; further, they do not help Christians in the realization of the truth that makes them free—what Jesus conveyed. If we are to preach (or share) Christ's Gift to us, our concern should be *how* we are to explain the Way of Christ so that Christ's contribution toward a free humanity is clear. A necessary question arises: What is it that preaching adds to the gospel? For, regardless of the gospel's message (the good news), a person can turn away from Christ out of a bad experience with a preacher. That is, a person may reject Christ and his teaching not due to fair reasons (e.g., not feeling the call, disagreeing with some principles of the Christian path, etc.) but because of a preacher's judgmental attitude, weak morality, or dogmatism. Claiming to represent Christ while making people bound and not free is far from the truth of Christianity, following *Christ's logic* that the truth will set us free. Thus, a question that any preacher needs to face is this: Should I talk or just get out of the way and give the gospel to be read instead?

But judgmental attitudes, weak morality, and dogmatism are not the only tendencies we should be warned against when preaching. There are

36. John 3:22–26; 4:1–2.

other problems with preaching that become more prominent within collectives—specifically crowds. Certainly, both preachers and devout Christians should be mindful of the powerful dynamics of crowds[37] or large gatherings—of their effects on emotion and feeling (e.g., inducing euphoria)—and not confound them with the power of Christ, the Light of being that gives everlasting peace regardless of context. We must remember: Christ Jesus' teaching was about truth and freedom. We are to gain experiential autonomy in God; spiritual fulfillment and true divine ecstasy are possible in solitude, even when a modest community may help us grow in experience and responsibility. Christ presented an understanding of life that would make our existence whole; in such wholeness, faith can awaken and healing can happen, but the emphasis is on wholeness and the freedom found in it. It is the spoken Word—the teaching of Christ—that makes a person see that Christ Jesus is the "Savior of the world."[38] Those who understand what they believe in are those who pay attention to Christ's teaching and know God because of it.

7. The Logos

Jesus said, "You will know the truth, and the truth will set you free."

Christ Jesus gave a teaching through which we could know the truth. The truth that Jesus talked about is not a truth subject to opinion; it is different from the prevailing understanding of truth today—"Something may be true for you, but not for me." The truth that Jesus talked about cannot be contained in a set of beliefs either—it is not a truth to be simply stated, agreed upon, and then asserted or imposed (some Christians seem to understand it in that way). In contrast to relativistic and dogmatic mindsets, Jesus' teaching points toward the experience of existential truth—the Truth

---

37. See the thought of Aldous Huxley on this matter—"crowd-delirium" as a form of "downward self-transcendence." He states: "'Where two or three are gathered together in my name, there is God in the midst of them.' In the midst of two or three hundred the divine presence becomes more problematical . . . tens of thousands, the likelihood of God being there, in the consciousness of each individual, declines almost to the vanishing point . . . Herded into mobs, the same men and women behave as though they possessed neither reason nor free will" (Huxley, *Divine Within*, chap. 12 ["Substitutes for Liberation"]).

38. "They said to the woman, 'We no longer believe just because of what you said; now we have heard for ourselves, and we know that this man really is the Savior of the world'" (John 4:42).

of being—which is neither an opinion nor a dogma. Jesus said, "I am the way and the truth and the life. No one comes to the Father except through me. If you really know me, you will know my Father as well. From now on, you do *know* him and have *seen* him" (John 14:6-7, emphasis added). Hence, the Father can be *known* and *seen*; and the Father is the Universal Spirit, the Absolute, the (nonrelative, nondogmatic) Truth of being. But the truth is also the Christ—the Logos, which comes from the Absolute and is thus the way to it. Accordingly, Christ (as Logos) has the power to regenerate our being, leading to a coherent form of existence in which we are capable of knowing the truth regardless of opinions and dogmas (i.e., besides sets of beliefs[39]), experiencing freedom through him.

Christ's teachings were given for a new relationship with God, inclusive of all Life, in a New Earth. The ancient sages knew of the freedom found in the Absolute, but their freedom did not include all aspects of what we are as human beings.[40] Through Christ, the possibility of all aspects of the human being participating in the Absolute, and so a more comprehensive freedom, becomes possible. Christ is the eternal I AM: "before Abraham was, I AM" (John 8:58 NKJV). He brings to human existence a new teaching that shows freedom as known in Eternity. Indeed, Jesus said that some precepts of the Mosaic law were given in such a form due to the hardness of people's hearts at the time, but they were not reflections of the Eternal. He said: "Moses permitted you to divorce your wives because your hearts

---

39. Here, "sets of beliefs" refers to nonessential beliefs. Every Christian has faith in Christ and believes in the Resurrection, of course.

40. Many faith traditions, even before the Incarnation of Christ, sustained the possibility of realizing the Absolute through contemplative practice, existential inquiry, and the transmission of God realization from master to disciple. The emphasis of the ancient mystical paths (especially in India, for the Taoist path is different) was on the transcendental apprehension of the Absolute through the soul (*jīva*). The Way of Christ does not deny such apprehension but fulfills the promise of a further participation in God by including all aspects of being (even the physical body) in a fuller experience of God realization—through the Logos. Probably, the closer sage of India to Christianity is Sri Aurobindo (1872-1950), who proposed a *Triple Divine* akin to the Trinity and worked on physical transformation—the *supramentalization* of the physicality through the descent of the Divine Force. Sri Aurobindo affirmed that the aim of his integral yoga had not been considered before his time, specifically commenting on the Hindu and Buddhist paths, their aims being liberation and transcendence (*moksha, nirvāna*). In comparison with Christianity, Sri Aurobindo's work is more centered on the ups and downs of the Spirit, which is *homeomorphically equivalent** to Third Hypostasis phenomena. See Aurobindo, *Letters on Yoga*, vol. 1, 7-8, 377; also *Letters on Yoga*, vol. 2, 407. For an overview of his philosophy, see Aurobindo, *Life Divine*. (*Panikkar's term.)

were hard. But it was not this way from the beginning" (Matt 19:8).[41] Christ thus restored the wholeness found at the beginning in his condition as the Logos incarnate.

Teachings are words, words are ideas, and ideas are impulses within the Logos—the primordial Word. Christ said: "If you hold to my teaching, you are really my disciples" (John 8:31). Indeed: the teaching of the Logos must be *held* so that it has time to rearrange our being—it is a process from the primordial impulse to actuality, to Life.[42] Holding to Christ's teaching is most beneficial when *exploring* it (rather than studying it or repeating it); for exploration keeps us engaged through a living dialogue between the Word and being.[43] In doing so, we become liberated as we discover the Truth of being in the eternal I AM. Freedom is thus found in the fulfillment of the primordial aspiration of our being to be the means of our becoming in the exploration of truth, in Eternity. To express what we are—Love—is the ultimate freedom, the sublimation of all our desires, refined, into an uncorrupted, undisturbed, clear power ever abiding in Truth.

Truth

The concern of the Christian of today should be to develop a Christianity *recognizable to Christ*, not to Christians. It is thus necessary to foster an *exploratory Christianity* which embodies Christ's example of engagement with human life. This possibility is desirable, as Jesus did not give all the teachings in his time, neither did he guide to all the truth to be known. He said: "I have much more to say to you, more than you can now bear. But when he, the Spirit of truth, comes, he will guide you into all the truth. He will not speak on his own; he will speak only what he hears, and he will tell you what is yet to come" (John 16:12–13).[44] Thus, there are teachings and developments of Jesus' teachings to be discovered through the Spirit while

---

41. The Mosaic law was meant to lead to freedom, as the psalm reads: "I will walk about in freedom, for I have sought out your precepts" (119:45). And so, if Christ brings the fulfillment of the law, he also brings the fulfillment of freedom.

42. John 6:63.

43. "Holding" implies a constant engagement with Christ's teachings. A good way of assimilating the teachings is through exploration and honest inquiry.

44. The passage continues: "He [the Spirit of truth] will glorify me because it is from me that he will receive what he will make known to you. *All that belongs to the Father is mine. That is why I said the Spirit will receive from me what he will make known to you*" (John 16:14–15, emphasis added).

being sanctified by the truth.[45] They will still be Christian because they are inspired by the Spirit sent in Christ's Name, by the Father and the Son. And we will know they are true when (and only if) they set us free.

---

45. "*Sanctify* them *by the truth; your word is truth*" (John 17:17, emphasis added).

CHAPTER 6

God Is Spirit
The Experiential Fact of God

1. Spirit—the Real God

JESUS SAID, "GOD IS Spirit" (John 4:24 NKJV). There is no other definition of God given by Christ than this: Spirit. And so, what a Christian worships, according to Christ—the Son of God, the one who is "in closest relationship with the Father" (John 1:18 NIV)—is Spirit. Such is the foundation of the Christian faith; and such worship must be done, as stated by Christ, "*in* the Spirit and *in* truth" (John 4:24, emphasis added).

Hence, to have faith in God means to put our trust in Spirit. And when a Christian worships God, they shall remember that such worship implies their abiding "*in* the Spirit and *in* truth"—that is, one is to rest in the contemplation of the all-pervading Spirit and the truth revealed in its apprehension. Christians who practice in this way are "true worshipers" (4:23); furthermore, they are "the kind of worshipers the Father seeks" (4:23), according to Christ's own words. Thus, even when not knowing what Spirit is (not as yet), still it is better to trust in Spirit—the real God, according to Christ—than to hold to an idea of God or to entertain a mythic belief in God. For God is neither an idea nor a mythic belief. God simply *is*, beyond imagination[1] or any construction of reality, prior to belief and, indeed, prior to the belief in God, because God is the foundation of reality—Spirit,

---

1. Imagination, as visualization, may have a place in devotional practice, but *no* product of imagination or visualization can be said to be God—Spirit.

the Truth. Any god that is not Spirit does not represent the Christian understanding of God; for God is Spirit, according to Christ, the Son of God.[2]

2. The Fact of God

Jesus said: "God *is* Spirit" (John 4:24 NKJV); "his worshipers must worship *in* the Spirit and *in* truth" (John 4:24 NIV, emphasis added).

There is no need for defending the existence of God. God is "a given"—a fact. It was so for Christ Jesus, and it should be so for those who follow his Way. There is no need for arguing whether God exists or not, simply because God—Spirit—can be experienced by the human being. Just as sensorial perceptions (what we see, touch, and hear) are experiential facts—we accept their existence without justification—for Jesus, as for those who follow his Way, God is an experiential fact[3]—God is simply "there," as a phenomenological datum. Hence, to say "God *is* Spirit" is enough for Jesus. It shall be enough for us. Jesus had many experiences of God: the descent of the Spirit by the river Jordan; the heart apprehension of God as the all-pervading Spirit; the embodied Light of being (experienced in his Transfiguration).[4] All these experiences of God are facts for Jesus, and so they are destined to be facts for Christians as well.

---

2. The inquiry of this chapter presents *kataphatic theology* (i.e., theology focused on what God is: Spirit) as complementary to *apophatic theology/via negativa* (focused on what God is not—e.g., thoughts, sensorial perceptions, etc.). Such an integrative avenue is not new. For example, Augustine explores the Trinity as what God is, while also inquiring into what God is not: "the Trinity is the one, the only, the great, the true, the truthful God, Truth itself . . . let no one think of any kind of contact or embrace in space or in place, as though there were three bodies, nor of any knitting together of a joint, as the fables relate of the three-bodied Geryon, but let us reject whatsoever may occur to the mind that is of such a sort" (Augustine, *On the Trinity*, 6).

3. For an experience to be *a fact*, it does not need to be the experience of every human being. That many people do not see God does not make God less of an experiential fact of human existence; for there are many who see God, each person to the extent of their capabilities, among other factors.

4. Quite different are the "demonstrations," so to speak, of Jesus as Messiah: the healing of the sick, the casting out of demons, the walking on water, the resurrection of Lazarus. Such demonstrations made many believe in Jesus. Yet, the question of whether Jesus is the Messiah is different from the question of whether God is a fact of human existence. There are no "demonstrations" of God but only testimonies of the reality of God—based on direct experience. Referring to his three-day entombment and Resurrection, Jesus said that "no sign will be given . . . except the sign of the prophet Jonah" (Matt 12:39 ESV; see also Matt 16:4; Mark 8:12; Luke 11:16–32). But such is the sign of

Consequently, discussions regarding the existence of God should be irrelevant for the Christian—they are based on ways of looking at life that are different from Christ's standpoint. That is, for Christ, God is the inherent foundation of reality, the most immediate and obvious truth; God is what makes life real, promising, and meaningful. This being so, Christ focused on revealing the experience of God—by seeing God, transmitting God (Spirit), teaching the Way of God, and doing what the Father willed and commanded him.[5] There was no need to find proof of God or to discuss God's existence.[6] Jesus said: "The work of God is this: to believe in the one he has sent" (John 6:29). That is: the work of God is to believe in Christ Jesus, the one who reveals the experience of God, being "in closest relationship with the Father" (John 1:18). Consequently, the answer to questions regarding the existence of God should not be "God exists *because* this or that";[7] the "answer," if any, to those who seek a proof of God is the assertion of *the experience of God*. It is not necessary to present evidence of God's existence, because God is self-evident as he *is*. Just as we know that thought is real—by experiencing it as *rational human beings*—likewise, we know that God is real—through experience as *God-conscious human beings*. And so, there is no reason or cause for God to be: God simply *is*.

God, being an experiential fact of existence, needs to be *realized*; entertaining ideas about God is not enough to live *consciously* in God. And God can be *realized*—apprehended—because God is the foundation of being and also of awareness. Yet sadly, Christians do not give much value to the experience of God nowadays; some think in quite utilitarian ways: "If believing in God is enough to feel secure, why to aim for something more?" "If God, as an idea, instils morality in society, why not embrace 'God' (as an idea) for this reason alone?" However, justifying God by some convenient function is not aligned with the Way of Christ. This type of thinking makes the reality and experience of God to be secondary for the Christian. We must remember that God is *truly real*. God is not an idea,

---

Jesus as Messiah, not the sign of God being real—as an experiential fact. Demonstrations never seem to have been sufficient for the Pharisees to believe in Jesus; instead, they were seeking to kill him (even so, some Pharisees eventually became believers [Acts 15:5]).

5. John 14:31.

6. 1 Tim 1:4–5.

7. God *is* prior to causation; God cannot be conditioned—explained—by a cause (a "*be-cause*"); see section 7.

however convenient it might be.⁸ God is God—Spirit. God does not need to be invented or defended, but simply apprehended.

3. The New Worship according to Christ

Jesus said: "God *is* Spirit"; "his worshipers must worship *in* the Spirit and *in* truth."

Before Christ, the worship of God was split. Those who knew God—the Jews,⁹ according to Christ—preferably worshiped in Jerusalem. Those who did not know God worshiped in their holy places. Yet, both worshiped God in a particular place of worship and depended on a custom and habit of worship. Jesus introduced a New Worship, which he explained to a Samaritan woman thus: "Woman . . . believe me, a time is coming when you will worship the Father neither on this mountain nor in Jerusalem. You Samaritans worship what you do not know; we worship what we do know, for salvation is from the Jews. Yet a time is coming and has now come when the true worshipers will worship the Father *in* the Spirit and *in* truth, for they are the kind of worshipers the Father seeks. God is spirit, and his worshipers must worship *in* the Spirit and *in* truth" (John 4:21–24, emphasis added). Jesus then disclosed to the woman that he is the Messiah—"I am he" (4:26), he said.¹⁰

Therefore, Christ Jesus expounded the nature of the New Worship to a Samaritan woman in Sychar¹¹—not to a man, not to a Jew, and not in

---

8. Even if one claims that the idea of God arises because God is real, it does not follow that God is an idea; God is God—Spirit—not the idea of God.

9. In a general sense, according to Christ Jesus, "the Jews" knew God (John 4:22). Yet, not all the Jews truly *knew* God: those who accused Jesus of being demon possessed, for example, did not know/perceive God (see *ginōskō*, "to perceive . . . to understand" [Mounce, *Interlinear New Testament*, 1035]), while Jesus certainly knows God (see *oida*, "to know" [Mounce, *Interlinear*, 1122]). Jesus states: "Though you do not know [perceive, understand (*egnōkate*)] him, I know [*oida*] him. If I said I did not, I would be a liar like you, but I do know [*oida*] him and obey his word" (John 8:55). See also John 8:19; 14:9; Acts 28:26–27.

10. See John 4:25–26. When Peter states that Jesus is the Messiah, Jesus asks the disciples not to tell anyone (Matt 16:20; Mark 8:30; Luke 9:21). Jesus will be formally condemned by the Jewish authorities when he confirms that he is the Messiah by replying, "I am" (Mark 14:62; see also Matt 26:64; Luke 22:70). Thus, for Jesus to reveal to an unknown Samaritan woman that he is the Messiah is an exceptional event—an act of trust and Grace, and a blessing to the New Worship.

11. A town in Samaria.

Jerusalem.[12] And such an event was recorded in Scripture because of the significance of the New Worship, given together with the proclamation beyond the Jewish community of Jesus as Messiah. The New Worship *of* Spirit and *in* the Spirit (i.e., abiding in the Spirit and not being separate from it) is to be practiced from the times of Jesus by all human beings, beyond gender, race, culture, and place.[13] With the New Worship, Christ Jesus challenged the idea of a culturally bounded God—a God inherited (given to us by generations past). He made what God is—Spirit—the center of worship, regardless of traditions and tales. In sum: Jesus said there was a time coming in which the God known to his people (the Jews) would be worshiped "*in* the Spirit and *in* truth"; then, the true worshipers would realize that their communion with the Living God is not confined to Jerusalem or to any physical location, nor ought to be limited to their kin. For God is Spirit and does not exclude places or races.

Consequently, the New Worship has four characteristics. First, *God is known*; for Christ says, "We worship what we do know"; Christians are to worship the God that is knowable and reveals himself as the perceivable foundation of being. Second, *God is Spirit*—not an idea, not an accumulation of ideas, not a social construction, not a personal imagination; the God that is known is, simply and straightforwardly, Spirit. Third, *the worship of God is done in the Spirit*; one realizes that God is Spirit in the surrendering of one's self entirely to what God is, so as to abide in the Spirit, worshiping from this perspective.[14] Fourth, *the worship of God must lead to communion with truth*. Being so, the New Worship must remove hypocrisy,

12. Jesus' disciples "marveled because Jews were not allowed to converse publicly with a woman, and a Samaritan at that. Jesus' words and actions transcend ethnic and gender-related customs of the time" (Gillquist, *Orthodox Study Bible*, 222; boldface removed).

13. "But you will receive power when the Holy Spirit comes on you; and you will be my witnesses in Jerusalem, and in all Judea and Samaria, and to the ends of the earth" (Acts 1:8). In the account of Christ's Transfiguration (Luke 9:31), the use of the word *exodon** in the context of the conversation between Moses, Elijah, and Jesus connects with the idea of "an exodus from Jerusalem, in which He [Jesus] will deliver mankind from the slavery of the evil one" (Gillquist, *Orthodox Study Bible*, 162). The New Worship is aligned with Christ's Transfiguration and Office, having effects beyond the confines of Jesus' ministry in Galilee, Samaria, Judea, Perea, Decapolis, etc., and, of course, Jerusalem. (*See *exodos*, "*a way out, a going out . . . departure, the exodus,* Heb. 11:22; met. *a departure* from life, *decease, death,* Lk. 9:31" [Mounce, *Interlinear New Testament*, 1063].)

14. Paul declares: "'For in him we live and move and have our being.' As some of your own poets have said, 'We are his offspring'" (Acts 17:28).

deceptiveness, and unrighteousness, for truth is opposite to these tendencies.[15] Therefore, if hypocrisy, deceptiveness, and unrighteousness persist, it indicates that the worship one practices is still the old, not the New. The new worshipers worship what God truly *is*, now and eternally: Spirit. They do so in the Spirit, beyond place, custom, and kin. These are the kind of worshipers sought by the Father, according to Christ.

4. What God Is

Jesus said: "God *is* Spirit"; "his worshipers must worship *in* the Spirit and *in* truth."

What God is, in reality, is a question clearly and openly answered in the New Testament. There is no need for Christians to guess and wonder what God is. The definitions of God in the New Testament are three: God is Spirit; God is Light; God is Love.[16] The first definition—God is Spirit—is given directly by Christ; the other two are given by John, who testifies about the revelation of God as Light and Love through Christ. God also has qualities—he is wise, holy, great, good—but these qualities are not descriptions of what God is. God is Spirit, Light, and Love, together—the Trinity. Spirit refers, first and foremost, to the Father, the Absolute—the First Aspect (Hypostasis) of the Trinity—but includes the entire Trinity as well. For "Spirit" is the Universal Spirit (the Father) but also the Personal Spirit (the Son), and the Spirit Force (or Holy Spirit); all three Aspects are "Spirit"—God. The other two definitions of God—Light and Love—refer to the Second and Third Aspects (Hypostases) of the Trinity: Light refers to the Son; Love, to the Holy Spirit. Nowhere in the New Testament, God is defined in any other way. What God is, according to Christian Scripture, is Spirit, Light, and Love.

God is a fact of human existence. Spirit, Light, and Love are not theoretical definitions of God; they refer to actual experiences of God. These definitions, recorded in Scripture, have been corroborated by those following Christ's Way to its experiential end. That is, God, from the beginning of Christianity, has been revealed as the Absolute, the Light of being, and the Spirit Force (i.e., the Divine Power, or Love)—all direct experiences for

---

15. On false worship, Christ quotes Isaiah: "This people honors me with their lips, but their heart is far from me; in vain do they worship me, teaching as doctrines the commandments of men" (Matt 15:8–9 ESV; see Isa 29:13).

16. John 4:24; 1 John 1:5; 1 John 4:16.

those who practice the New Worship "*in* the Spirit and *in* truth," as given by Christ. This is the consistent and recurring testimony. Complementarily, the revelation of God is at times associated with particular events. Such events have played a prominent role in the history of Christian experience: the descent of the Spirit on Jesus in the River Jordan, subsequently given to many; the Transfiguration, in which the glorified Christ gave testimony of the nature of the Light of being and of the light kingdom; the Resurrection, which made physical divinization a visible fact, from then on becoming constitutive of the Christian aspiration; the coming of the Pentecostal Fire, sent in Christ's Name, which aligned Christian existence with the Life made possible through Christ's Office; manifestations of Christ's Being (e.g., Christ Events or Pauline Events), which give testimony of the continuing presence of Christ.

What God is, in actuality, is not for us to judge and demarcate. God reveals himself in sentient creation, and we—sentient human beings—report the way God is revealed to us. We are not to define God beforehand, nor limit God in any way. If our ideas of God—our philosophies, our theologies, our beliefs—cannot accommodate how God reveals what God is, we shall change them accordingly. For God does not change his nature to accommodate our ideas. And it is not a task for Christians to battle on ideas about God but to worship God "*in* the Spirit and *in* truth," acknowledging the ways God reveals himself. God is an experiential fact of existence, which has been recorded in Scripture and in other Christian texts (e.g., the writings of the fathers, the saints, and the mystics) from the beginning of Christianity. The Living God is thus truly real, as testified by direct experience, regardless of our ideas and beliefs about God. God has been known openly in Christianity as Spirit, Light, and Love. Even so, some Christians still do not know it.

5. Words and Divine Cognition

Jesus said: "God *is* Spirit"; "his worshipers must worship *in* the Spirit and *in* truth."

The meanings of the words "God" and "Trinity" are loaded with collective and individual contents; because of it, people have mixed feelings toward them. These feelings, sometimes negative (at times due to traumatic experiences), do not belong to God and Trinity; that is, the collectively and individually shaped words "God" and "Trinity" are not God and Trinity in reality. Yet, loaded words can hinder our worship of God. Further, many people nowadays do not resonate with the word "God" anymore, or do not accept it as equal to "Spirit,"[17] rejecting prayer and the worship of God only for that reason.[18] Some say that "in any case, Jesus never uttered those words" (for he spoke in Aramaic). However, the problem with these faith words is not that Jesus spoke in the context of a people for whom the Aramaic words for God, the Father, the Son, and the Holy Spirit had a particular connotation—a feeling and undertone—we can only guess today. The real problem lies in emphasizing words over experience, for we may have lost the language in which Jesus spoke, but we have not lost the experience he conveyed. Christ's New Worship—"*in* the Spirit and *in* truth"—establishes our being in God and Trinity; in doing so, it breaks through the collectively and individually shaped meanings of these words as they are confronted with the real experience they are meant to convey. Thus, through the New Worship, the words "God" and "Trinity" are freed from their hindering history; consequently, they can better represent the revealed reality of what God is—Spirit, Light, and Love—as apprehended by Christians.

Christianity shall emphasize the New Worship of God instead of the belief in God;[19] for the New Worship brings people to God, while the advocacy of believing in God often puts up barriers to realizing the God who is—the foundational reality of being. In emphasizing and practicing the New Worship, the word "God" becomes as fitted to represent the real God as the Aramaic word for God that Jesus used. Likewise, the word "Trinity" (a word that Jesus never used[20]) becomes fitted to represent what God, in

---

17. See the term "spiritual but not religious" (SBNR). According to the division between spirituality and religion that this term suggests, some people may argue that Christianity is mostly religious but not spiritual—in contrast to Buddhism, for example, which could be more easily both.

18. Words, in general, are not perfect reflections of what they represent—"God" and "Trinity" are not God and Trinity in themselves, and an inquiry into the origin of these terms helps only partially to reach our ends. That is, etymological analysis may aid through a temporary redirecting of attention (toward a closer-to-truth meaning); however, such analyses are not the main tool in the understanding of terms that represent Ultimate Reality—God.

19. Emphasizing the belief in God, in practical terms, is not the same as emphasizing the belief in Christ Jesus. The emphasis of Christianity should be on the belief in Christ (through a proper understanding of the Atonement and Resurrection), but also on the experience of God—the Trinity.

20. At least, considering the Gospels' accounts.

the New Testament, is: Spirit, Light, and Love. As the words "God" and "Trinity" are freed from their loaded meanings through the New Worship, we must also free these and other faith words from the products of collective and individual imagination. Particularly, Spirit, Light, and Love describe the reality of God as experienced in the New Worship; they are *not* objects of worship to be represented by images of God. Indeed: God is Spirit—the Consciousness that abides in all; God is Light—the foundation of Life; God is Love—the dynamic Force of creation and growth. These are descriptions of God as revealed in the New Worship, not an object of worship to be imagined in any way.

To worship God "*in* the Spirit and *in* truth" thus frees our understanding of God from collective and individual contents and from all imaginations while in worship, leading to the experience of the Trinity as an experiential fact of human existence.[21] God is an experiential fact because all Aspects of God—the Trinity—can be apprehended in the conditions we live in. Further, all Aspects of God—Spirit, Light, and Love—are coessential: they can be experienced simultaneously in divine cognition. This is the reason why the Trinity is God and not three gods; certainly, the statement "the Trinity is God"[22] is an experiential fact as well. Through divine cognition, the divinization of human nature becomes possible.[23] As the human being is capable of apprehending their own divine nature in relationship with both the Divine and the Earth, the promise of a New Earth is beheld.[24]

---

21. Richard Rohr has made important contributions to moving, in his own words, "doctrine and dogma to the level of inner experience." Rohr suggests that the rediscovery of the Trinity is essential—"important and timely at this very moment in history"—for three reasons: (1) the Trinity "offers us a much deeper phenomenology of our inner experience of Transcendence"; (2) it is useful to dialogue with other faith traditions and with science; (3) it provides a more complete understanding of Christ (i.e., of Christ Jesus, and not just Jesus) (Rohr, *Divine Dance*, 124, 121–22).

22. One *ousia*, three *hypostases*. That is: one God/essence; three Aspects of (the) Trinity—Spirit, Light, Love. The three Aspects do not belong to God but rather *are* God. Likewise, the three Aspects do not belong to (the) Trinity but *are*, together, (the) Trinity.

23. On Christian divinization, see, for example, Symeon the New Theologian, *Discourses*; Palamas, *Triads*.

24. A major contribution to this realization is that of Raimon Panikkar, who proposed a nondualistic relationship between the Cosmos/World (*Kosmos*), the Human (*Anthrōpos*), and the Divine (*Theos*). Panikkar called such a realization the *cosmotheandric intuition/experience/vision* (a "cross-cultural interpretation of the [theanthropocosmic] invariant," which refers to the ordinary awareness of these three realms). Through the *cosmotheandric experience*, human beings come to realize their existential role as Mediators between the Divine and the World (i.e., "Man as a *pontifex maximus* who

It is upon this realization that the Christian sees that Jesus' promise of inheriting the Earth lies not in waiting for a future event but in the *work at present*, through the conscious participation in a light kingdom which is both coming and emerging in the instant that one lives.[25]

6. The Fact of God Remains in a Heartbreaking World

Jesus said: "God is Spirit"; "his worshipers must worship *in* the Spirit and *in* truth."

God is known through direct experience in the practice of the New Worship. Without such worship, what God is remains unclear, and so Christian faith becomes fragile—prompt to either dogmatization or rebuttal. Faith in God is sometimes lost in sight of the unfairness of the world. The argument is straightforward: "In the world, there is unjustifiable suffering—murder, abuse, rape, torture, injustice, inequality, hunger—but a fair God would not allow such sorrows; a fair God would act in the face of unfairness and make the world fair." The heartbreaking realities of our world should indeed make those who believe that "the hand of God is behind everything" *tremble*. If a baby is born in a war zone and a bomb falls into her home: What kind of God would allow such things to happen within his own creation to those made in his image and similitude? This question and others like it are disturbing to those who do not practice the New Worship, to those who hold to *ideas* of God still not knowing the God they worship. Certainly, the realities of the world are a strong argument against some *ideas* of God, and many lose their faith because of it.

Those who worship "*in* the Spirit and *in* truth," however, do not deny God because of any argument whatsoever: they know that the God they worship is the undeniable foundation of being. Thus, true worshipers

---

enthrones Matter"; "Man, that Mediator between Heaven and Earth"); see Panikkar, *Rhythm of Being*, 269, 278, 285–86, 303–4, 263–367 (entire discussion). The *cosmotheandric experience* represents a call to work toward a New Earth with a solid foundation on direct mystical experience. Certainly, Panikkar's theological propositions are not apart from his own direct mystical experiences. In his diaries, he writes: "I am radically changing my vision of reality—expressed too cryptically in the *cosmotheandric vision*. God as Separate Entity does not exist. Such is the Trinity—that I believe I live. It is the reality of the Spirit—which is not my ego, but which is neither separate nor separable from me. Jesus is the Christ, the fully deified man" (Panikkar, *Diaries*, 306; emphasis added [entry: Tavertet, March 17th, 2007]).

25. See chapter 10, where this understanding is further developed.

(those sought by the Father, according to Jesus) do not lose their faith in God because of the suffering and unfairness of the world. The logic is simple: the Spirit did not descend on Jesus while he was living in a fair and loving world, nor was Jesus transfigured into the Light in an idyllic and luminous world; the experience of God was possible in the unfair world that Jesus inhabited, just as it is possible in the unfair world that we inhabit today. Jesus said that the works of the world are evil;[26] yet, works that are evil do not—cannot—prevent God from manifesting himself in the world. Hence, the true worshipers of God, through their experience of God, bear witness to the fact of God *in the face of* human suffering and the unfairness of the world.

God—Spirit, Light, and Love—is the foundation of being, the basis of Life as experienced in the New Worship. For those who experience God in this way, there is *no need* to believe in God as a controlling entity (i.e., as "a being" above who governs everything in either mechanistic or humanlike manners). Fairness and justice in the world are possible, but they need to be fought for; the human being is responsible for and a participant in the bringing about of fairness and justice, being part of the new creation *already*. If some Christians believe in a deterministic cosmos—that all events are caused by God—that is their assumption: they will have to explain how the heartbreaking realities of the world fit into their idea of God. The perspective of those who practice the New Worship is different: just as the man born blind is not responsible for his misfortune (nor are his parents), yet in his misfortune "the works of God might be displayed" (John 9:3) (Jesus says),[27] Christians should know that God is not the cause of misfortunes, yet often the Grace that is revealed in their surrender during tribulation. The Light which emanates in the darkest hours of our lives when the self surrenders to the silence of being—that is God. There is evil in the world, and the works of the world are evil,[28] but God is not the cause of evil. Christians are to see God beyond cause and effect, beyond the need for a fair and perfect world, to realize Grace regardless of conditions. Thus, the fact of God as a noncausal yet graceful reality remains, even in a heartbreaking world.

---

26. "The world cannot hate you, but it hates me because I testify that its works are evil" (John 7:7). On being the object of hate by the world/people, see Matt 24:9; Mark 13:13; Luke 21:17; John 15:19.

27. See John 9:1–7.

28. John 7:7.

God Is Spirit

7. Reason, Science, and God

Jesus said: "God *is* Spirit"; "his worshipers must worship *in* the Spirit and *in* truth."

Without an understanding of the ways we can use reason in regard to God, it is difficult for a rationally oriented person to accept God. Simply put, there is conventional reason, for which two apparently opposing essentials (e.g., existence and nonexistence) cannot be at the same time; this type of rationality focuses on dualisms (it is built on them) and is not well equipped to discuss God. There is another type of reason—divine reason—that emphasizes complementarities; according to it, existence and prior-to-existence (or potential existence) can be simultaneously. Divine reason describes the reality of God—Spirit—as an experiential fact of existence in which being (to-be) is not opposed to its negation (not-to-be), because "not-to-be" means potentiality-to-be (i.e., potential being). This is the reason why mystics and sages have always attested to nonexistence,[29] vacuity, no-self, and a truth prior to being (the substratum of all), even when referring to an existing reality—God—and a Divine Life to be attained by *being*.

Also, a proper understanding of God—as an experiential fact—is much needed to address some forms of skepticism. For, a person asserting that God does not exist often does not deny Spirit but rather an *idea* of God which does not represent the reality of God as an experiential fact. That is: "God does not exist" truly means "I do not believe in your idea of God—in what believers believe"; but it does *not* mean "The experience of God is not real." Certainly, God, as an experiential fact, is a reality acceptable to reason: reason is not against experience; further, reason can actually aid in the understanding (and integration) of the experience of God. And so, when a person argues, "God cannot be real *because* so-and-so," they are not addressing the reality of God—the fact of God—for there is not a cause for the real God to be. That is, there is not a "be-cause" (a cause-to-be) that makes God reasonably real or unreal. God is Spirit, a fact of conscious existence—the truth in which being and prior-to-being coexist.

---

29. Such is the path known as *via negativa* in Christian mysticism, which emphasizes the Father (the Absolute) as the entry point to knowing God. *Via negativa* is an example of *apophatic theology* (i.e., theology focused on what God is not) and is complementary to *kataphatic theology*, which, focusing on what God is, tends to emphasize the Trinity and also existence (i.e., "being") from the beginning of the path.

Today's dispute about God's existence is mostly driven by the science-versus-religion debate; it is (probably has always been) a political debate: a quest to free science from the scrutiny, at times oppression, of institutionalized religion—not a thorough inquiry into truth. And so, even when left unsaid, freedom to pursue knowledge and explore human life without the control of religious authorities (and to keep it that way) is the core concern of the secular scientific world when posing both reasonable and unreasonable arguments against religion, and consequently against the idea of God (the assumed foundation of religion). But the science-versus-religion debate is not about the reality of God. Indeed, the phenomenological facts of God—Spirit, Light, and Love—are not a concern for those who criticize religion.[30] Many scientists and even some critics of religion know the experiential fact of God to be true and engage in the New Worship themselves. And there are dialogues between science and religion that do acknowledge the fact of God as well. The experiential facts of God as apprehended by human beings reflect the reality attested in Scripture—God is Spirit, Light, and Love. This reality is revealed to those who practice the New Worship regardless of place, race, and culture, and also regardless of their scientific and religious mindsets.

Truth

God is Spirit, an experiential fact of existence; God must be lived. Jesus pointed in that direction when introducing the New Worship: "God *is* Spirit"; "his worshipers must worship *in* the Spirit and *in* truth." No longer is there a place for naïve ideas about God. In the New Worship, God is real and can be apprehended, with absolute certitude, as the very foundation of being.

---

30. Critics of religion focus on the fundamentalist traits of institutionalized religion and persisting ideas of God that are not free from the influence of the Greco-Roman tradition. Certainly, a Zeus-like god is very different from Christ Jesus' definition of God: Spirit.

CHAPTER 7

They Will Inherit the Earth
On Forgiveness and Meekness

1. The Blessed

JESUS SAID, "BLESSED ARE the meek, for they will inherit the earth" (Matt 5:5).[1]

The New Earth will not admit pride: the intensity of the power of the Divine will not be possible to bear with a prideful heart. Those who think of themselves as strong and proud today will become fragile then, when the time of the meek comes. Some believe meekness weakens a person. Yet, it is the attribute of those who embody the power of God. Meekness comes with inner surrender and the capacity to serve what is important to Life; it favors a state of joyful calm and serenity found in a relaxed chest and a gentle heart.[2] Meekness is not for those who listen to the world—to the changing fashions and the societal pressures of today—but for those who listen deeply to the presence of the Divine. Indeed, there is a formidable power latent in God, awaiting; it can be felt, and its guidance allowed, through the meekness of being. The commitment of the meek is not the same as that of the enlightened sages—those who have attained spiritual Liberation from the Earth. The meek do not seek Liberation but give testimony of the Living God on Earth; they are committed, in their surrender, to take part in

---

1. See Ps 37:11 and Luke 3:5 ("Every valley shall be filled in, every mountain and hill made low"). See later note on the word "meek" (*praus, praeis*) in Matt 5:5.
2. These are effects of the *lowliness of self*.

human destiny. The new heart is a humble heart, and those with a humble heart will inherit the New Earth.

2. Lightness of Being

Jesus said, "Blessed are the meek, for they will inherit the earth."

Humbleness is an important trait of the Christian heart. Jesus said: "Come to me, all you who are weary and burdened, and I will give you rest. Take my yoke upon you and learn from me, for I am gentle and humble in heart, and you will find rest for your souls. For my yoke is easy and my burden is light" (Matt 11:28–30). Christ is meek (i.e., inwardly gentle), and his humble heart gives rest and unburdens those who follow him. Christians should welcome such a gift from Christ—their burden should be light; they should consequently give rest to others as well. However, some Christians seem to be carrying a heavy burden (even in a self-righteous way); it is reflected in their heavy-felt humbleness and also in their unrest, for burden, humbleness, and rest are related, as Christ said. Differently, Christ Jesus' humbleness, coming from the Spirit's descent, makes one lowly, light, and rested in communion with the Divine. Such Christ-like humbleness is neglected today. The result is the perpetuation of heavy-felt humbleness, which comes from focusing on one's own faults, producing shame, and also repressed anger, with disastrous results when it can no longer be contained. Indeed, in the Christian culture we have inherited, it seems as if a Christian is more of a Christian by being sinful and remaining burdened by sin; the redemptive, regenerative, and transformative functions of Christ and the Spirit are not so obvious (have we become numb to them?). Sadly, for some Christians today, one is humbled by shame, not by the Spirit's descent.

Those who bear a heavy burden think of sin as caused by a corrupted human nature, thus emphasizing the need for constant repentance; they follow John the Baptist words: "You brood of vipers! Who warned you to flee from the coming wrath? Produce fruit in keeping with repentance" (Luke 3:7–8).[3] On the other hand, those who embrace the possibility of being humbled by the Spirit, as taught by Christ, understand that sin is ignorance in the absence of Light; that sin is overcome by Light. These two views are not the same. We must choose. Just as John the Baptist preceded Christ—the Son of God, whose sandals John was not worthy to untie and

---

3. See Acts 19:3–5.

carry[4]—likewise repentance precedes the Light. Christians are not to keep on emphasizing repentance as if the Light has not come. John the Baptist said it himself: "He must increase, but I must decrease" (John 3:30 ESV). Thus, the focus of Christianity should be the Light; for the Light brings humbleness in alignment with Christ, whose "yoke is easy," and whose "burden is light."

The Christian call to humbleness should unburden Christians, uplift them, and make them joyful in their progress in Christ. Jesus said: "Whoever humbles himself will be exalted" (Matt 23:12 ESV); "Whoever humbles himself like this child is the greatest in the kingdom of heaven" (Matt 18:4 ESV). Darkness can be, and should be, acknowledged, never denied; but it should be acknowledged in the lightness of being and the transparency of the self. From this perspective, darkness can be freed with patience, understanding, and love. Problematically, Christianity remains heavily dogmatic and judgmental. Also, many Christians conform to being "sinners," not aspiring to grow out of their sins; hence, their burden is heavy—not light like that of Christ and those who follow his Way. But if humbleness is a quality of Christians, it should be of such characteristics that make a person feel light. Indeed, Christ emphasized lightness of being, making people free in the Light that he is, and they are as well, through him—"You are the light of the world" (Matt 5:14), he said to those who were to bear witness to him. In the face of sin, Christ offered not despair but hope.

3. The Two Doors of Forgiveness

Jesus said, "Blessed are the meek, for they will inherit the earth."

The sign of a meek person is a humble and forgiving heart. However, forgiveness is broader than just the forgiving of someone or something. Truly, forgiveness has two doors—forgiving and asking for forgiveness; and the second (asking for forgiveness) is perhaps more fundamental in the work for the light kingdom. Since what would be more beneficial for society—if everyone would forgive or if everyone would ask for forgiveness? It is asking for forgiveness that transforms the world into a divine world, for asking for forgiveness interiorizes lowliness, leading to divine embodiment and a more radical transformation of society. Even so, forgiving (not just asking for forgiveness) needs to be put into practice as well; our freedom depends on it. Hence, forgiving and asking for forgiveness have

---

4. Matt 3:11; Mark 1:7; Luke 3:16; John 1:27.

complementary[5] effects: forgiving leads to liberation, asking for forgiveness to calmness and belonging to the Earth. Indeed, forgiving opens the heart to the freedom of the Eternal—the Infinite—while asking for forgiveness favors the Divine's descent.

A humble and forgiving heart, with practice and perseverance, eventually reveals forgiveness beyond individual acts of forgiveness as a *state of being*. That is, the heart of the meek, as the understanding of the nature of forgiveness matures, does not look into particular events but inhabits existence as if forgiveness were a continuum in which single acts have little importance. Although people tend to think of forgiveness in relation to individual acts and particular events—of forgiving someone for something, of being forgiven for something we have done—Christ's teachings lead to recognizing forgiveness as a state that we inhabit. Certainly, when Christ encourages us to forgive "up to seventy times seven" (Matt 18:21–22 NKJV),[6] he is suggesting a particular predisposition toward forgiveness (a persistent attitude) which leads to the realization of forgiveness as a *state of being*. This is Christian wisdom: forgiveness is an unremitting necessity (mistakes are done and suffered every day); because of it, forgiveness should be part of the automatic operations of the self, far from our constant efforts either to forgive or to ask for forgiveness. Consequently, so that the teaching of Christ may grow and give fruit, forgiveness—both forgiving and asking for forgiveness—must develop from punctual, extraordinary acts to habitual acts (as Paul suggests[7]) and, even further, to the realization of forgiveness as a *state of being*.[8]

The emphasis on forgiveness and meekness is a major contribution of Christ to the heart of humanity and to human friendship. These two attributes—forgiveness and meekness—must be kept together: while forgiveness makes possible the stabilization of the power of the meek (i.e., the

---

5. Forgiving and asking for forgiveness are complementary in the Lord's Prayer; see Matt 6:12; Luke 11:4. See also Matt 6:14–15; 18:35.

6. Other translations have opted for "seventy-seven times" (NIV, ESV). In any case, probably Jesus does not mean that forgiveness is to be relinquished once a certain number of acts of forgiveness is reached—he is pointing to unlimited acts.

7. Eph 4:32; Col 3:13; 2 Cor 2:5–11.

8. I have explored the possibility of experiencing *forgiveness as a state of being*, corroborating its liberating and appeasing potential before making this claim. A practical exploration of this topic led to the development of a *yoga of forgiveness*—a path of divine communion through forgiveness, maybe unique to Christianity and its message; see Portilla, *Yoga del perdón*, 46–47, 111–24.

Spirit needs proper conditions to descend), meekness creates the context for forgiveness to flourish. The centrality of forgiveness and meekness in Christianity provides companionship and friendship also in social enterprises. Without forgiveness, communion among fellows is not possible; neither is growth, for any mistake causes resentment—it becomes an event in history rather than a breeze passing by. The heart of the meek cannot be well-balanced without forgiveness—it is crucial to transcend egotism and self-centeredness by considering the importance of our communion with the whole. Forgiveness is fundamental in the interiorization of Christ's teachings, setting the human heart into an entirely different relationship with others and with Life.

4. Forgiveness and Gratitude

Jesus said, "Blessed are the meek, for they will inherit the earth."

Christ planted the seeds of forgiveness as a crucial stepping stone in humanity's advancement. First, he gave a basic understanding directed to God-fearing people who sought the forgiveness of God. He said: "And whenever you stand praying, if you have anything against anyone, forgive him, that your Father in heaven may also forgive you your trespasses" (Mark 11:25 NKJV); and he continued, "But if you do not forgive, neither will your Father in heaven forgive your trespasses" (11:26 NKJV).[9] That is, one was asked to be forgiving before asking for God's forgiveness; to repent was not enough to be forgiven by God—one must be forgiving of the doings of others as well. The same principle is found in the Lord's Prayer, as given by Christ: "And forgive us our debts, as we also have forgiven our debtors" (Matt 6:12).[10] Thus, in order to be forgiven by God, one is asked to forgive others in the first place.

Such an emphasis was necessary among a people who feared God more than loved God.[11] Certainly, some of Christ's disciples had been followers of John the Baptist; since their prior concern was to avoid divine punishment,

---

9. In a similar line, see Matt 6:14–15; 18:32–35. These sayings present God's forgiveness as being conditional: if a person does not truly forgive, the Father will not forgive that person. It implies that *without forgiveness* (an attitude in alignment with Love and Grace) *only the principle of Justice—accountability for all deeds—would apply*. See chapter 8, section 4, on Justice and Love.

10. See also Luke 11:4.

11. "Surely his salvation is near those who fear him, that his glory may dwell in our land" (Ps 85:9).

they would have been slower in witnessing the Light and assimilating into the Way of Christ. Further, Jesus presented his understanding of forgiveness in a time when forgiveness, even to a loved one—a "brother or sister" (Luke 17:3)—was rare, and it had to be taught.[12] Jesus said: "If your brother or sister sins against you, rebuke them; and if they repent, forgive them. Even if they sin against you seven times in a day and seven times come back to you saying 'I repent,' you must forgive them" (17:3–4). This statement may appear as nothing extraordinary to some: many forgive loved ones not only when they repent but when they do not repent as well. Yet, Christ's teaching is not about simple acts of forgiveness; it suggests patience in being forgiving—forgiveness as a *state of being*.

Still further, Christ demonstrated another form of forgiveness on the cross. He said: "Father, forgive them, for they do not know what they are doing" (Luke 23:34). Through these words, Jesus showed that the forgiveness of God may occur even without the fear of God and the repentance of those to be forgiven, through the Grace that Christ brought.[13] Such forgiveness suggests an additional possibility for Christians who seek oneness with the Heart of Christ: being compassionate and forgiving toward those who "do not know what they are doing."[14] And such graceful forgiving applies to asking for forgiveness as well. That is, as we ask for the forgiveness of those who "do not know what they are doing," we may ask for being forgiven for the suffering we cause in our ignorance (i.e., for the harm *we* do not know *we* are inflicting). If so, forgiveness becomes larger: we are forgiving and asking for forgiveness for things we know and also for things we do not know.[15] Finally, by becoming aware not only of the suffering that one creates but also of its inevitability, the Christian starts appreciating

---

12. Even if Jesus refers in Luke 17:3–4 to major wrongdoings and not to minor, daily faults in thought and deed, the need for explaining that one should forgive a "brother or sister" who sincerely repents seems to indicate that the norm was not forgiveness (i.e., forgiveness was not a given at the time).

13. John 1:17.

14. Some may think that Christ did not forgive in this occasion—that he just asked the Father to forgive. Yet: How is the Father to forgive and not Christ, who is the Son of God, thus one with the Father?

15. We can ask for forgiveness not just for the things we know but also, out of a deeper empathy and insight, for the things we do not know. Certainly, there is suffering created by thoughts, feelings, and actions of ours that we may not remember or know. Also, we may forgive thoughts, feelings, and actions of others against us that we do not remember or know. Both mechanisms are part of the internal operations of *forgiveness as a state of being*.

their position in existence as a *privileged* sentient being for whose spiritual growth much suffering is endured.[16] Upon this realization, asking for forgiveness is transformed into *gratitude*, and meekness seems the only way to be attuned to what is given—Life.

5. Earth—Home of Divine Descent

Jesus said, "Blessed are the meek, for they will inherit the earth."

The descent of the Spirit began upon the Baptism of Christ in the River Jordan. It activated mercy in the upper regions of the mind and meekness in the chest and heart. The descent of the Spirit is not the same as the ascent of the Spirit. The ascent of the Spirit was already accessible to the ancient sages before Christ—by raising their consciousness, they were able to touch the Divine Light above, attaining Liberation from the Earth. With the descent of the Spirit, Jesus showed a new way of inhabiting and relating to the Earth: earthly existence, from then on, was realized as both desirable and willed by God. Also, from the very beginning, the Spirit was given in the open to anyone accepting the faith.[17] Thus, the ancient connection with the Divine above, traditionally accessible to a few through the Spirit's ascent, became possible for the many through the Spirit's descent. And so, unlike those who sought Liberation from earthly existence, Christ asked the LORD: "My prayer is not that you take them out of the world but that you protect them from the evil one" (John 17:15). The descent of the Spirit was to transform the relationship between human beings and earthly existence. Indeed, Jesus' disciples were "the salt of the earth" (Matt 5:13).[18]

---

16. For a further exploration of these themes, see Portilla, *El yoga del perdón*.

17. John 3:22, 26. In a short time, Jesus and his disciples had baptized more individuals with Spirit than John the Baptist with water (John 4:1–2). Such a promptly given Initiation—in the Spirit, by the Spirit—would be unthinkable in the ancient traditions, in which only highly accomplished practitioners were able to experience glimpses of Divinity after a tedious process of discipleship.

18. A further sanctification by the Fire of Life would follow after his departure. Jesus said: "Everyone will be *salted with fire*. 'Salt is good, but if it loses its saltiness, how can you make it salty again? Have salt among yourselves, and be at peace with each other'" (Mark 9:49–50, emphasis added). Further, foreseeing the coming of the Fire of Life (starting at Pentecost), Christ said: "I have come *to bring fire* on the earth, and how *I wish it were already kindled*! But I have a baptism to undergo, and what constraint I am under until it is completed!" (Luke 12:49–50, emphasis added).

Thus, the destinies of the human being and of the Earth have been intimately related from the time of Christ.[19] Even so, human beings have developed a dysfunctional relationship with the Earth. It reflects the prevailing worldviews of today: some think that the Earth was given to humans for its exploitation; others think that humanity is a burden for the Earth (i.e., humans are destroyers who deplete resources, extinguish species, and devastate natural beauty); restoration of an almost human-less natural environment is their ideal. Such views do not grasp the profound connection between the human being and the Earth in their shared destinies. The Christian understanding should be different: if the Earth is to be inherited, as Christ said, it is because the Earth is the *destined home* of the divine kingdom. As the Spirit descends upon the human being, the destiny of the human being is changed, and so the destiny of the Earth is changed as well; more so if the Earth is apprehended by the human being as the seat of the kingdom of heaven.

Christ established the conditions for humanity to realize the promise to Israel: that "the meek shall inherit the land and delight themselves in abundant peace" (Ps 37:11 ESV). With Christ, the promised land became the Earth, and the chosen people became humanity. To bring the gospel to humanity implies that the Earth should be cared for—it is the inheritance of the meek and the place where the kingdom is realized. The meek are not removed from their inheritance—they cherish it, respect it, and nurture it spiritually. Indeed, the Spirit descends in the meek, and so they contribute, through their divinization, to the divination of the Earth.[20] As for those who are prideful—either spiritually or in a worldly way—they resist the coming of the kingdom, for pride involves self-inflation, self-centeredness, and self-feeding (including the abuse of others and of the Earth); all these tendencies are against the Spirit's descent and its effect—meekness. Hence, the proud are not fitted for environments where the light kingdom consciously emerges. Meanwhile, the meek serve and give themselves in service. Only the meek will have lasting peace on Earth.

---

19. Upon the Atonement, the "veil" which divided worldly existence and the Divine was torn, just as the veil in the temple was torn (Matt 27:50–51 NKJV).

20. See notes on Christian divinization and Panikkar's *cosmotheandric experience* in chapter 6, section 5.

6. Entering Jerusalem

Jesus said, "Blessed are the meek, for they will inherit the earth."

The one day Christ Jesus was celebrated in the open was the day he entered Jerusalem. "'Hosanna to the Son of David!' 'Blessed is he who comes in the name of the Lord!' 'Hosanna in the highest heaven!'" (Matt 21:9),[21] cheered the crowds to welcome their Savior. And the one quality chosen to signify Christ's message, in this crucial moment, was meekness; its symbol, a donkey.[22] Jesus entered Jerusalem sitting on a donkey—not on a horse, not on the shoulders of his followers. For lowliness is where the power of God resides, and pride what the power of God eludes. It fulfilled the words of the prophet Zechariah: "Say to Daughter Zion, 'See, your king comes to you, gentle and riding on a donkey, and on a colt, the foal of a donkey'" (Matt 21:5).[23] Sitting on a donkey was a gesture toward the meek—those who best represent the kingdom; it was also the exemplification of how those who hold true divine authority are to present themselves.

But meekness is not so well understood today: it should not be confounded with a person being kind and polite in all circumstances.[24] It is clear in the Bible that kindness and politeness are not the right reading of Christian meekness and of the character of the meek. Jesus himself, having entered Jerusalem as the embodiment of meekness, goes immediately to the temple and rebukes the money changers and the merchants overturning their tables.[25] That is, Jesus, in his meekness—in his receptiveness to

---

21. See also Mark 11:9–10; Luke 19:38; John 12:13.

22. Meekness is an attribute consistent with Christ's words and actions throughout his ministry.

23. See Zech 9:9. (John 12:16 explains how the disciples did not understand the signs at the time.)

24. The Greek term *praus* appears in the sayings regarding meekness (Matt 5:5; 11:29; 21:5). See *praus* ("*meek, gentle, kind, forgiving*, Mt. 5:5; *mild, benevolent, humane*, Mt. 11:29; 21:25") in Mounce, *Interlinear New Teatament*, 1148. In some versions of the Bible, and depending of the verse, it has been translated as "gentle," which is acceptable if referring to an inner gentleness as opposed to inner hardness or heaviness. Yet, nowadays, the word "gentle" seems to be too much associated with outer expressions—with being simply nice or polite. It is thus difficult for it to be understood as "meekness," which in the Gospels is compatible with harsh forms of outer conduct, as portrayed in the cleansing of the temple.

25. This is the second recorded episode of the cleansing of the temple, described in Matt 21:12–17; Mark 11:15–18; Luke 19:45–48. In Mark, it says that it occurred the day after the entry into Jerusalem, while in Matthew and Luke it is not specified. The first episode of the cleansing of the temple is described in the Gospel of John, occurring at the

the Spirit and the will of the Father—does not hesitate; he storms into the temple reproaching both doers and enablers. Hence, Christian meekness is the conduit of a will which does not conform with kindness and politeness in the face of unrighteousness. A mistaken understanding of meekness and an improper allocation of power in society make the Christian hesitant in conceiving meekness as an attribute that gives authority; correcting this mistake is urgent. It is said that Moses, with all his might and strength, was "very meek, more than all people who were on the face of the earth" (Num 12:3 ESV). And Jesus, who came to fulfill the law of Moses, was not only meek, but he brought meekness to a further degree, also giving the Spirit to those willing to receive it. (These individuals who received the Spirit became meek as well through it.)

Therefore, meekness is not an attribute that denotes weakness. Meekness is needed for Divine Power to descend and become stabilized; then the power of the meek can be manifested—by surrendering to the Spirit and the will of the Father. Jesus demonstrated meekness in words and actions, being uncompromising with the truth. He was rejected and hated by the world not because he was weak but because he was as powerful as he was meek. Further, he warned his disciples that they would be rejected and hated by the world as well, not because of their weakness but because of their witness to the truth in their meekness—in their surrender to God. Indeed, the promise for the meek is to inherit the Earth—the New Earth—not the world, which hates the meek. Christians have lost power in their readings of Christ, which conform too much to the culture of today; this attitude is not adequate, for the world still represents an old human enterprise too much influenced by the unrighteous and the proud. Hence, the distinctiveness of Christian meekness needs to be reconsidered once again.

7. The Meek Can Be Taught by God

Jesus said, "Blessed are the meek, for they will inherit the earth."

Jesus showed how meekness leads to ultimate surrender to God, and how such surrender serves to usher in the coming of the kingdom: Jesus surrendered to the healing works of the Father, and through them he gained the trust of the people;[26] Jesus surrendered to the commandment

---

beginning of Christ's ministry (John 2:13–21).

26. See, for example, John 5:1–20, 36.

of the Father to speak,[27] and because of it he gave a liberating teaching to humanity; Jesus surrendered to his death on the cross,[28] and through it he gave Atonement and the Resurrection to the faithful. Jesus, through his surrender, time and again put himself at risk—doing works of healing on the Sabbath, revealing his status as the Messiah,[29] challenging the culture in which he lived; in his meekness, he offered little human resistance to the Father,[30] leaving no way but the Way as he exemplified it.

The ways of the meek are different from the ways of the proud; the power of the meek is not the same as the power of the proud either. To turn the other cheek, for example, is an action of the meek which comes as an alternative to the way of the proud: "Eye for eye" (Matt 5:38–39).[31] To turn the other cheek can shame the wrongdoer, but, more importantly, it may cause their *spiritual transformation*. Even so, the gesture must come through surrender to the Spirit, not by strategy or choice. That is, to turn the other cheek is not a prescription for the Christian but a possibility in following the Way of Christ; it requires great self-giving and trusting God's ways toward justice. What Jesus demonstrates with his teachings and gestures is not a submissive attitude in the face of evil and violence, nor abandoning the hope for justice,[32] but an uncompromising look toward the Truth of being, which challenges instinctive self-protective reactions. For example, when Jesus is stricken while he is being interrogated, he questions the man immediately: "If I said something wrong . . . testify as to what is wrong. But if I spoke the truth, why did you strike me?" (John 18:23).[33]

---

27. John 12:49.

28. Matt 26:38–46; Mark 14:32–42; Luke 22:41–44.

29. The risk was not only because of what Jesus, the disciples, or the Samaritan woman could say in relatively safe contexts; even those from whom Jesus cast out demons would start saying that he was "the Christ, the Son of God!" (Luke 4:41 NKJV), and he had to silence them.

30. We know of Jesus' hesitation at the Garden of Gethsemane before the Passion, which shows how Christ Jesus is truly human and not only divine.

31. "Eye for eye" mirrors the law of cause and effect yet involves taking effects into one's own hands in a negative way—revenge, retaliation. There is no Grace in pursuing this path. This topic is also addressed in chapter 5, section 3 and chapter 7, section 7; see also chapter 8, section 4.

32. On hope for justice see, for example, the parable of the persistent widow in Luke 18:1–8.

33. This event happens before Annas, "the previous high priest, the power behind the religious establishment"; he then sends Jesus to Caiaphas, who "was high priest that year" (Gillquist, *Orthodox Study Bible*, 260; boldface removed).

The wrongdoer is thus confronted with truth. Jesus' reaction is neither retaliation nor passivity; further, Jesus, in his meekness, may have brought *spiritual transformation* to the violent official.[34]

There is much to be gained through meekness because the meek can be guided and taught by God. The meek can understand what the works of God are because the meek are fine-tuned by God through the working of the Spirit in them. The proud, on the other hand, learn little from God, even if they assert they do; only by much suffering—their own and the suffering they inflict on others—the proud eventually learn something: that their way is not the Way. The woes of Christ are directed to the proud precisely: the privileged and reverenced hypocrites who "do all their deeds to be seen by others" (Matt 23:5 ESV) ("Woe to you Pharisees, because you love the most important seats in the synagogues and respectful greetings in the marketplaces" [Luke 11:43]);[35] the "experts" who stopped learning long ago and prevent others from learning as well ("Woe to you experts in the law, because you have taken away the key to knowledge. You yourselves have not entered, and you have hindered those who were entering" [Luke 11:52]);[36] the authorities, the "blind guides" who focus on the insubstantial and neglect the substantial, thus leading the corruption of the world ("Woe to you, teachers of the law and Pharisees, you hypocrites! You give a tenth of your spices—mint, dill and cumin. But you have neglected the more important matters of the law—justice, mercy and faithfulness. You should have practiced the latter, without neglecting the former. You blind guides! You strain out a gnat but swallow a camel" [Matt 23:23–24]).[37]

Truth

The New Teaching is a teaching for the meek. Only the meek have ears to hear; only the meek have the patience to hold to the teachings of Christ. The meek will persevere and see their hearts transformed—through the Spirit's descent. Subsequently, they will become carriers of the Mystical Cross in

---

34. The Spirit prompts Jesus' active response—the use of words that induce self-awareness. Increasing self-awareness is what prevented the stoning of the adulterous woman as well (John 8:3–11) and, in general, is the effect produced in the audience of many sayings of Jesus.

35. See also Matt 23:6–7.

36. See also Matt 23:13.

37. See also Luke 11:42.

communion with the indwelling Logos on Earth. In them the Spirit will live, and they will witness the light kingdom so that Jesus' saying is fulfilled: "Blessed are the meek, for they will inherit the earth."

CHAPTER 8

Take What Is Yours and Go Your Way
On Fairness and Justice

1. Abundance in Heart

JESUS SAID IN A parable, "Take *what is* yours and go your way. I wish to give to this last man *the same* as to you" (Matt 20:14 NKJV).[1]

To "take *what is* yours" and, simply, "go your way"—not comparing yourself to others—results in liberating freedom. It is the freedom of those who decide to live, modestly, a life of abundance in heart. To experience such a freedom is difficult, for the mind is constantly comparing this to that instead of looking at how "this" (i.e., what we already have) may be fair already, regardless of what "that" might be. A tormented mind looks at the past and says, "I was stupid, I should have asked for more" or "I was deceived; I could have paid less." This type of mind departs from a position of scarcity: one is poor and miserable always, regardless of one's wealth. A mind that reflects such tendencies takes away the possibility of living in freedom wisely, generously, and *fairly*! It also sets oneself apart from gratitude, which is found in living a simple, spiritual life. Thus, relinquishing unwise comparison is a major step to experiencing liberating freedom.[2]

---

1. These are the words of the landowner to the early workers in the parable of the workers in the vineyard (Matt 20:1–16); the words are directed to those complaining about receiving a pay they had actually agreed to.

2. I say "unwise," for not all comparison (just as not all judgement) is wrong: generosity often comes by comparison; we can learn much through comparative analysis as well.

Those who do their best, regardless of what others do, take what is theirs and simply go their way—those are wise; they have found "the road that leads to life" (Matt 7:14), and they live in abundance.[3]

2. The Fairness of the Just

Jesus said, "Take *what is* yours and go your way. I wish to give to this last man *the same* as to you."

These words are stated by the landowner in one of Christ's parables. The landowner had employed some workers early in the day for a day of work.[4] These workers had agreed to be paid a denarius; yet, at the end of the day, after comparing their effort to that of others who came later and were paid the same, they demanded more. The rationale of these workers is familiar: "I started my work early. I worked more hours than those who came later; therefore, I should be paid more than them." And so, even if the early workers had already agreed to be paid a denarius, they considered that the landowner should increase their pay; otherwise, the landowner would be unfair, according to their thinking. This logic appears to be founded on generally acceptable principles of fairness, but it is not—it privileges self-interested motives over agreements, promises, and covenants in life. The logic of the kingdom of heaven—the logic of Life—can only be reflected through a pure mind which, acknowledging the interdependence of human existence, is capable of respecting agreements, promises, and covenants; it is, therefore, a just mind. A worker with a pure mind would have thought: "I agreed to a pay (a denarius). I did the agreed work. I was paid what I agreed to. Therefore, the landowner is fair." (For Jesus' parable is *not* dealing with the problem of the exploitation of workers.)

The teaching of Christ's parable is this: be truthful to your word and do your duty; there is no need of comparing yourself with others when you understand the importance of respecting agreements. Those who think like the complaining workers are not autonomous in God: they do not have a word in which others can trust, for they themselves do not trust their own judgment when entering into an agreement. Those with a pure mind

---

3. The ways of God are *not* those of the many: "Enter through the narrow gate. For wide is the gate and broad is the road that leads to destruction, and many enter through it. But small is the gate and narrow the road that leads to life, and only a few find it" (Matt 7:13–14).

4. See the entire parable of the workers in the vineyard (Matt 20:1–16).

respect what they agreed to—they are "just" in that sense; they seek *fairness at the beginning* so that they do not have to look for it afterward.[5] Conversely, those who are like the complaining workers do not seek fairness at the beginning—they look at how much they can get at any given point in time, regardless of the agreements they have made; in that sense, they are "opportunists." Indeed, the fairness of the just is based on commitment, while others seek opportunity.

The various agreements between the landowner and the workers in this parable reflect the logic of the kingdom of heaven. Those who came later and, trusting the landowner, agreed to be paid "whatever is right" (Matt 20:4) were given the same as everybody else. They were even paid before those who were first: "So the last will be first, and the first will be last" (20:16). Hence, there is a great difference between our culture and that of the kingdom of God. The landowner replied to the complaining workers: "I am not being unfair to you, friend. . . . Are you envious because I am generous?" (20:13, 15). Likewise, the kingdom of God appears unfair to those who are envious and do not let go of their self-concern. Those who ponder the time they have worked and the heat they have endured (in the field or in life) ask themselves: "Why should the last be the first and get an equal reward in the kingdom of heaven?" They assess the fairness of the landowner—God—instead of appreciating his generosity. The attitude of the Christian should be different from that of the complaining workers: they should *praise* the generosity of God (and of others as well), *respect* their own agreements, and *move on* with their lives.

3. Finding Fairness in Asking

Jesus said, "Take *what is* yours and go your way. I wish to give to this last man *the same* as to you."

Those who pray usually do not think about the fairness of what they ask—they pray for what they pray, not considering if what they ask for is fair. Moreover, one does not ask God to be fair. One does not pray, "Give us such-and-such, but only if it is fair" or "May Thy kingdom come, yet only if it seems fair to Thee." For the fairness of God is considered to be certain. Surely, prayer assumes the generosity of God; also, that what is

---

5. Jesus is *not* talking about cases where one is clearly cheated or forced to accept certain working conditions, *nor* about historically inherited inequality (e.g., the gender pay gap).

given with generosity is fair. Should we assume that *sincere* prayer makes a person generous and fair? When we see injustice in the world, we may pray that it be remedied, but the world needs to change just as much as humanity's heart. This is the reason why praying sincerely to God is necessary—it instills generosity and fairness in the human heart. As our heart becomes more generous, we become fairer; the world becomes fairer as well, because the world reflects our common heart. This is how fairness is found in asking—by becoming generous in the likeness of God.

Those who ask in Christ's Name "will receive" (John 16:24); Christ himself said so.[6] But asking is not only about receiving—it implies the giving of one's self, generously, in a variety of ways. First, there is the giving of one's self in faithful prayer, for Christ said that what is asked for is given through faith.[7] Second, there is the giving of one's self by overcoming shyness, shame, and the embarrassment of asking, just as the two blind men who wanted to receive their sight had to persevere: "Lord, Son of David, have mercy on us!" (Matt 20:30), they shouted at Jesus despite the crowd rebuking them; so, they received.[8] Third, there is the giving of one's self to uncertainty and challenge, because there are some requests made in prayer that could demand much if granted. For example, when James and John asked to be seated next to Christ Jesus in the kingdom of heaven, they were immediately questioned about whether they would be willing to endure Jesus' same path—to drink of the same cup and be baptized with the same baptism.[9] Hence, asking the Divine implies the giving of one's self with generosity, requiring courage to assume the consequences. (Prayer with a proper understanding is a *courageous adventure*!)

Of course, one may not receive what is asked for. Yet, asking often reveals that one's longing is different from what one thought it to be: it is not the receiving of something but the surrender of one's wishes to the divine will in the service of the kingdom. The everyday prayer "Thy will be done"[10] is a powerful statement of faith that reflects such longing. "Thy

---

6. See Matt 7:7–12.

7. Matt 17:20; 21:21; Mark 11:23; Luke 17:6; 18:1–8.

8. See Matt 20:29–34. When Jesus gave them sight, they followed him, for their longing was to be with Christ. See also how a paralytic was brought to Jesus in a bed from a roof (Mark 2:3–5).

9. Mark 10:35–44; Matt 20:20–28. The request of James and John had consequences, even when what they had asked for was not for Christ to give.

10. A statement following Matt 6:10 or Luke 11:2, yet not necessarily uttered as part of the Lord's Prayer.

will be done" means the following: "Notwithstanding anything I may pray for, desire, or will, may Thy will prevail; and if there is any conflict between what I pray for, desire, or will and Thy will, then Thy will shall prevail; and if Thy will is for me to endure challenges that I have not prayed for, desired, or willed, I accept Thy will in my surrender to Thee." Those who do not want to do or endure what they do not pray for are like the complaining early workers in the parable—they want to know the conditions of prayer beforehand, and even when what they prayed for is granted, they are often dissatisfied. Those who understand the statement of faith "Thy will be done" are like the workers who came later and trusted the landowner (i.e., God). Christians pray for many things; some of them are granted, but when some of them are not, there are those who think that their prayer has lost power, that they lack faith, that God does not listen to them. Do they ever ask themselves the consequences of daily praying "Thy will be done"?

4. Justice and Love

Jesus said, "Take *what is* yours and go your way. I wish to give to this last man *the same* as to you."

There are two principles that need to be studied together—Justice and Love. The principle of Justice[11] guarantees equilibrium in existence; it gives rise to the laws of cause and effect and the movements of reciprocity, compensation, return, and repayment.[12] The principle of Love guarantees growth and evolution; it gives rise to the laws of Grace and the movements of generosity, forgiveness, charity, and mercy.[13] Grace grants the possibility of rising from fallen conditions in which no repayment is possible; indeed, when everything seems to be lost, there is still hope in the Love of God. The parable of the workers in the vineyard portrays the complementarity of Justice and Love: The saying "take *what is* yours and go your way" represents the fairness of God—his respect toward agreements. The saying "I wish to give to this last man *the same* as to you" represents God's generosity toward those who trust in him.

---

11. Deut 32:4; Pss 7:11; 11:7.

12. See, for example, Job 4:8; Ps 126:5; Matt 26:52; Luke 6:37–38; Gal 6:7; Rev 22:12–13.

13. Just on "mercy," see, for example, Exod 33:19; Pss 4:1; 6:2; etc.; Matt 5:7; 9:13; 12:7; 23:23; Mark 5:19.

Take What Is Yours and Go Your Way

The Old Testament emphasizes Justice; the New Testament emphasizes Love: "For the law was given through Moses; grace and truth came through Jesus Christ" (John 1:17); and "God so loved the world that he gave his one and only Son" (3:16). Certainly, before Christ's Incarnation, the relationship with God was dominated by the principle of Justice. The Israelites feared God and aspired to live a righteous life, hoping to see God's judgment and Justice. "Let the Lord judge the peoples. Vindicate me, Lord, according to my righteousness, according to my integrity, O Most High" (Ps 7:8), prays the psalmist; and this was their belief: "I know that the Lord secures justice for the poor and upholds the cause of the needy" (Ps 140:12).[14] However, because God's judgment operates beyond the span of one human life, the Israelites struggled to understand God's Justice. Prophet Habakkuk states: "Why do you make me look at injustice? Why do you tolerate wrongdoing?" (Hab 1:3).[15] One had to accept that even a righteous man, like Job, could pass through tremendous difficulties and challenges, sometimes greater than those suffered by the unrighteous: "He destroys both the blameless and the wicked" (Job 9:22), says Job.

Christ Jesus challenged explanations based only on Justice (and so on cause and effect) with Love and Grace.[16] He saw in hardships not a punishment for past wrongdoings but an opportunity for Love, and thus a context for Grace. When his disciples were discussing whether a man could be born blind because of sin (that of the man or of his parents), thinking in terms of Justice and cause and effect, Jesus challenged their views by introducing Love and Grace: "Neither this man nor his parents sinned . . . but this happened so that the works of God might be displayed in him" (John 9:3). And he concluded, "While I am in the world, I am the light of the world" (9:5), subsequently healing the man.[17] Certainly, without accepting Love and Grace, the mind is repeatedly trapped in trying to find a cause for all the happenings of life, and so it often errs: it sees punishment where there

---

14. Also: "For the Lord will not reject his people; he will never forsake his inheritance. Judgment will again be founded on righteousness, and all the upright in heart will follow it" (Ps 94:14–15).

15. See also Hab 1:13; Isa 59 (59:9 in particular).

16. Justice is causal: it reflects the consequences of deeds, the balance which comes through things that can be often observed and judged; it appears to be predictable (to some extent). Love is acausal: it is given without reasons; its effects are almost always surprising in their unpredictability. This is one of the reasons Jesus' replies and actions are always surprising and unpredictable.

17. John 9:1–12 (entire passage).

is a condition for Love (as with the man born blind); it seeks justification in disasters (like the fall of the Tower of Siloam) when the call is to repentance to receive the Grace of God.[18] The fourth and fifth beatitudes refer exactly to these two principles—Justice and Love: "Blessed are those who hunger and thirst for righteousness, for they will be filled. Blessed are the merciful, for they will be shown mercy" (Matt 5:6–7). Thus, both Justice and Love will be fulfilled in the emerging kingdom of God.

5. Christ—the Judged Who Is to Judge

Jesus said, "Take *what is* yours and go your way. I wish to give to this last man *the same* as to you."

With Christ, the *Word of the Lord* once given as the laws of righteousness[19] becomes Word *as* Being, Light, and Life.[20] Righteousness is fulfilled with Christ Jesus as the experience of Grace in *just being*. The Christian realization regarding righteousness is this: we did not know that the depths of the Grace of God were deeper than those of God's righteousness, but now we know it.[21] Hence, with Christ we came to know the profundity of God's Love. If people mostly feared God before Christ, with Christ people realized that the human soul was deeply loved by God. For this reason, a Christian could love God naturally, peacefully, and trustfully[22]—love toward God was revealed as being more fundamental (i.e., primordial) than fearing God and his judgment. Hence, the almighty God became servant of his own creation through Christ because of the profundity of his Love. Such is the Christian conclusion: the beauty that the Father saw in the human

---

18. Luke 13:2–5. Jesus is very clear in that those killed by the fall of a tower in Jerusalem, in the neighborhood of Siloam, were not worse than others. He further calls all to repentance so that they do not "perish" (probably referring to spiritual death rather than physical death).

19. On *the Word of the Lord*: "All your words are true; all your righteous laws are eternal" (Ps 119:160); "Your word is a lamp for my feet, a light on my path. I have taken an oath and confirmed it, that I will follow your righteous laws" (Ps 119:105–6).

20. John 1:1–14.

21. John 1:14–17.

22. To love God was necessary before the times of Christ (see Deut 6:4–5; Matt 22:35–40; Mark 12:28–31; Luke 10:25–28). Yet, with Christ it becomes *a matter of course*—an effortless outcome of following the Way.

being made him give his beloved Son[23] so that a Divine Life on Earth could be possible—through redemption and regeneration in Christ.[24]

Christ—the Logos made Man—is the Light; as such, he is also the judgment of the human being. That is, Christ is not made judge out of his own volition; but he is "the judgment" in his very nature as the Light. It is written: "Everyone who does evil hates the light, and will not come into the light for fear that their deeds will be exposed" (John 3:20). "This is the verdict" (3:19), so the Gospel says.[25] Thus, evil is judged—exposed—in the Light. Christ Jesus is also the Son, who exercises judgment in accordance with the will of his Father, God; for he states: "I can do nothing on my own. As I hear, I judge, and my judgment is just, because I seek not my own will but the will of him who sent me" (John 5:30 ESV). Hence, Christ Jesus exercises judgment as both the Light and the Son—by his nature and in his surrender to his Father. Conversely, Christ Jesus is judged and condemned, having to endure much pain. And so, the absolute fairness made manifest in Christ—by being the Light and doing the will of God—meets the absolute unfairness of humanity's judgment toward Christ. In the Passion, Jesus endures the pain of unfair judgment penetrating all aspects of his humanity: he is falsely accused, mistreated, insulted, tortured, mocked, spit upon, crucified (among thieves), and killed in front of his mother. Because of it, he can show ultimate empathy and compassion toward those who are unfairly treated in this world—his judgment will never be without understanding.

Christ is judge, for the Father "has entrusted all judgment to the Son" (John 5:22).[26] Thus, Christians should beware of what Christ criticized the most: hypocrisy.[27] Christ did not criticize people for not going to the temple or for not respecting the Sabbath; neither did he pay much attention to bypassing customs and traditions (the washing of hands, fasting, etc.). He did not criticize those things. Instead, Christ spoke against what today could be considered a self-righteous pharisaical Christian. Who a

---

23. John 3:16.

24. 1 John 4:9. Initial redemption leads to further regeneration of all aspects of the human being *through* Christ and *in* Christ.

25. See John 3:18–21.

26. See John 5:22–29; Matt 25:31–46; Rev 20:11–12. See also John on how the Holy Spirit, "the Advocate" (16:7) sent by Christ, proves "the world to be in the wrong about ... judgement, because the prince of this world now stands condemned" (16:8–11).

27. On hypocrisy, see chapter 3, section 5; also chapter 2, section 4; chapter 5, section 4; chapter 6, section 3; chapter 7, section 7.

self-righteous pharisaical Christian is today: a Christian who likes to be praised, and so prays to be seen in churches and on special occasions; a Christian who criticizes those who do not go to church on Sunday while failing to challenge temple-church malpractice;[28] a Christian who preaches self-restraint and family values but breaks the most basic rules of decency; a Christian who idolizes rules and social conventions and forgets to live by Love. Christ Jesus gave clear signs of what is most displeasing to his eyes and ears: not sin, but hypocrisy. Christ is merciful,[29] but he did not show mercy with hypocrisy—he exercised judgment on hypocrisy above all else. Christ's judgment criteria need to be understood through his own words and demonstrations, which speak heavily against self-righteous pharisaical tendencies then and today.

6. On (False Testimony by) Being Judgmental

Jesus said, "Take *what is* yours and go your way. I wish to give to this last man *the same* as to you."

Christians who are proud and judgmental give false testimony of Christ: they make cause for would-be Christians to turn away—to look for other ways of life. Some Christians feel proud even with little achieved—asserting their beliefs among believers and suggesting others to do the same. Christians who are proud and judgmental tend to ask similar questions to those they newly meet: "Are you a believer?" "Do you pray?" "Do you go to church?" They do not realize that these questions do not define the quality of a person in any meaningful and sensitive way. Such questions are usually asked by either naïve or pharisaical Christians—those who make central the unimportant and push what is important away.[30] It would be far better to ask how one deals with hypocrisy, as standing against hypocrisy is a faithful testimony of Christ—the one with authority to judge, and who does not stand hypocrisy.

Regarding our own judgments, we are used to thinking that we should abstain from harshly judging others, following two well-known sayings of Christ. The first saying—"With the measure you use it will be measured back to you" (Luke 6:38 ESV)—creates awareness of God's judgment. The second saying—"Why do you see the speck that is in your brother's eye,

---

28. See chapter 3, section 5.
29. Luke 6:36 (Christ is what he preaches—merciful, in this case).
30. Matt 23:23–24; Luke 11:42.

but do not notice the log that is in your own eye?" (6:41 ESV)—prompts self-awareness.[31] Both sayings indicate the need to be cautious when judging others. Additionally, we are inclined to think that the cautionary judgment of others applies only to negative judgments; however, positive judgments (e.g., praising others) should be considered as well. For a harsh, unfair judgment can cause an emotional wound to a person, but praising someone undeservedly can harm the person in a different way; that is, praising a person for their virtues, skills, or achievements yet not considering their need for developing character and whether their actions are oriented in the service of the kingdom can be damaging both spiritually and regarding worldly affairs (it could contribute to their downfall by increasing their pride). Therefore, unwise, unmeasured judgment is to be avoided, whether it is negative or positive (even if well-intentioned, of course).

Jesus generally neither condemned nor praised people but encouraged growth by always keeping in mind the demands of the light kingdom to come. He said: "Do not judge, and you will not be judged. Do not condemn, and you will not be condemned. Forgive, and you will be forgiven. Give, and it will be given to you" (Luke 6:37–38). Christ's teaching leads to a state of humbleness and communion with Life free from both exaltation and condemnation. Christ's concern is God's concern, and in God's eyes, people are not what they seem to be in the order of society. Matthew, being a tax collector, was counted among sinners in his society; yet, he was called to be an apostle by Christ.[32] Similarly, the tax collector who repents is justified before God, while the Pharisee who rejoices in his righteousness (comparing himself with others) is not.[33] "Those who exalt themselves will be humbled, and those who humble themselves will be exalted" (Matt 23:12), says Christ.[34] Christians who are proud and judgmental have not removed the log in their eye, but—*worst!*—they give false testimony of Christ, making would-be Christians turn away from God.

7. The Last Ones

Jesus said, "Take *what is* yours and go your way. I wish to give to this last man *the same* as to you."

31. See Luke 6:37–42; Matt 7:1–5.
32. Matt 9:9–13; Mark 2:13–17; Luke 5:27–28.
33. See the parable of the Pharisee and the tax collector in Luke 18:9–14.
34. See also Luke 14:11; 18:14.

Jesus' parable of the workers in the vineyard represents the ideal disposition of the human being toward economic life ("Take *what is* yours and go your way"), but it also explains the economy of creation: "So the last will be first, and the first will be last" (Matt 20:16). The human being is destined to be one with God, for the human being was made in the image and the likeness of God (Elohim).[35] Yet, being the last in creation, the human being must trust God, just as the workers who came last trusted the landowner. That is: there were workers who had agreed to a payment (and that was fine until they complained); there were workers who came later, and the landowner promised to give them "whatever is right" (Matt 20:4); but there were workers who came even later—*the last ones*—and they went to work by simply being told to "go and work" (20:7). In the same way, Christians must "go and work," trusting the fairness of God.

Trust is easier when one is generous. Christians are meant to develop a generous heart. There is no need for negative, unwanted comparisons when there is *abundance*—when those who have eyes to see can really see the inherited spiritual *abundance* and nurture it further. Jesus says: "Open your eyes and look at the fields! They are ripe for harvest" (John 4:35), for "the saying 'One sows and another reaps' is true" (4:37). Thus, eternal life brings together those who work with generosity (the "sowers") and those who honor that which has been done and build on it (the "reapers") "so that the sower and the reaper may be glad together" (4:36), as Christ says. Indeed, when the generosity of the "sowers" meets the appreciation of the "reapers," the question of "fair pay" ends; unwanted comparisons end as well. That is, there is no need for the landowner to say, "Take *what is* yours and go your way"; one finds harmony in the abundance of spiritual life, working with generosity for those who will come after while reaping the fruits of the labor of many who worked before with generosity as well. Hence, Jesus concludes: "I sent you to reap what you have not worked for. Others have done the hard work, and you have reaped the benefits of their labor" (4:38).[36] (This saying, so true for spiritual matters, would be applicable to worldly affairs as well.)

And so, the logic of the kingdom of God is based on *abundance*: "Whoever has will be given more, and they will have an abundance" (Matt 13:12).[37] And *abundance* leads to higher *demands*: "From everyone who

---

35. Gen 1:26–28; 5:1–3.
36. See John 4:34–38 (entire passage).
37. See also Mark 4:25; Luke 8:18; 19:26.

has been given much, much will be demanded; and from the one who has been entrusted with much, much more will be asked" (Luke 12:48). Finally, higher *demands* lead to higher *rewards*: "Those who are victorious will inherit all this, and I will be their God and they will be my children" (Rev 21:7). Thus, *abundance* leads to *demands*, and *demands* lead to *rewards*. And on *rewards*, Jesus said: "Whoever welcomes a prophet as a prophet will receive a prophet's reward, and whoever welcomes a righteous person as a righteous person will receive a righteous person's reward. And if anyone gives even a cup of cold water to one of these little ones who is my disciple, truly I tell you, that person will certainly not lose their reward" (Matt 10:41–42). Finally, of *heavenly rewards* we know this: The reward of a prophet is "great . . . in heaven" (Matt 5:12).[38] The reward of a person who, regardless of the circumstances, does what is right is to dwell in the "sacred tent" (Ps 15:1) of the LORD, to "never be shaken" (15:5); the reward of Christ is with him, and it is given according to what one has done.[39] In sum: in the kingdom of God there is not scarcity but *abundance*. *The last ones* will be the first to enjoy such *abundance*.

Truth

We should not complain of God's Justice, nor of the unfairness of the world: God is just beyond our limited observations; the world will be unfair in the face of our dislikes. There is equilibrium in Eternity—justice is done. There are also temporal degeneration and regeneration—they are part of the dynamics of growth.

Christ's kingdom will be established on Earth, yet it is not of this world—no society (or nation) is "fair" in the way that Christ showed. Envy is strong; it often overpowers the will to do what is right and to respect agreements in life. Hence, Love and Grace must enter the contemporary mind and culture; our societies need to understand how generosity is necessary for them to grow. An envious society must ponder Jesus' words: "Take *what is* yours and go your way." When people and societies *go their way*, it means that they have left their envy behind and accepted the generous wish of God: "to give to this last man *the same* as to you."

---

38. See also Luke 6:23.
39. Rev 22:12–13.

CHAPTER 9

How Can You Say, "Show Us the Father?"
On God Realization

1. Philip's Asking

REGARDING THE MYSTERIES OF the kingdom, Jesus has the hope that those following his Way will live such mysteries as he does.[1] A major mystery is that of seeing the Father. Jesus hopes that his disciples will see the Father because the apprehension of the Father is necessary for the kingdom of God to become factual.[2] When the apostle Philip asks him, "Lord, show us the Father and that will be enough for us" (John 14:8), Jesus replies, "Don't you know me, Philip, even after I have been among you such a long time?" (14:9). And he concludes, "Anyone who has *seen* me has *seen* the Father. How can you say, 'Show us the Father'?" (14:9, emphasis added).

Here, Jesus' hope that his disciples will see the Father[3] is confronted with the difficulty one faces when conveying such an important experience of God. Still, the mere asking of Philip is of great significance for the Christian Way. Philip's statement "That will be enough for us" means that

---

1. The Baptism of the Spirit Force is given from the beginning. This is the first mystery, but there are others: seeing the Father; knowing the Light of being; the Pentecostal Baptism (or Baptism of Fire); the bearing of the Mystical Cross.

2. Divine Existence implies a life truly lived, *consciously*, in God. See John 3:20–21.

3. Seeing the Father is necessary for giving testimony of the truth—to live in *conscious communion* with the Father and Christ is important for "bear[ing] much fruit" (John 15:8).

what the disciples mostly needed—what they were eager to acquire at that point above all else—was the direct experience of God, the Father, the Absolute. The disciples did not ask Jesus for further teachings on the kingdom but to simply and plainly *see* the Father. More importantly, Jesus' answer shows that seeing the Father is not only possible but, actually, *a matter of course*. (Jesus is not surprised by what he is being asked for, but rather is surprised that Philip is asking for something *they should already know*!) Philip's asking—"show us the Father"—testifies of the importance of seeing the Father in the Christian Way. Jesus *assumed* that those following his Way would see the Father—just as he saw the Father, just as they saw him.

2. Those Who See God Are Blessed

Jesus said, "Anyone who has seen me has seen the Father. How can you say, 'Show us the Father'?"

To see God is a blessing. Christ believed it to be so. "Blessed are the pure in heart, for they shall see God" (Matt 5:8 ESV), he said.[4] This saying is part of the Beatitudes; therefore, it is a central teaching of Christ. The Christian should thus have the aspiration to see God so as to obtain such a blessing in the Way of Christ. Also, seeing God implies knowing God better, and knowing God prevents us from hurting others, according to Jesus. He said: "The time is coming when anyone who kills you will think they are offering a service to God. They will do such things *because they have not known the Father or me*" (John 16:2–3, emphasis added). Therefore, seeing God is both a blessing and a necessity in the Way of Christ: a blessing, because seeing God instills bliss and peace in the human heart; a necessity, because seeing God prevents fundamentalism and hurting others.[5] When Christians say that it is not necessary to see God, they do not realize the

---

4. To see God implies knowing God through the soul and heart's mystical vision. It does not mean that one knows "all about" God but that one starts living consciously in God—learning God's ways in a more intimate and direct manner. God may be not-knowable through the ordinary senses, but he can be seen by the soul and experienced by being. Also, he may be not-knowable through the intellect, but seeing God informs the intellect: "We have the mind of Christ" (1 Cor 2:16), Paul says.

5. Seeing God must be combined with Christian discipleship (i.e., with holding to Christ's teaching) so that God is *truly lived*. One should not assume that mystical experiences in themselves prevent fundamentalism—mystics can be quite opinionated, bordering on obvious and subtle forms of fundamentalism at times.

consequences of following such a suggestion. The God who Christ knew and spoke of is a God that can be seen.

Still, some Christians attest proudly that because they believe in God, they do not need to see God, *as if not seeking to see God were a proof of their belief* (do they forget that the apostles, being faithful and believing, asked Jesus to see the Father, God?). Such Christians tend to mistake faith for belief—they do not understand that faith leads to seeing God, for God is the source of faith, just as he is the source of being.[6] Further, they often misunderstand the words of the resurrected Christ when he said to Thomas, "Blessed are those who have not seen and yet have believed" (John 20:29). For, Christ Jesus was referring to those who had believed in his Resurrection without the need of *seeing him resurrected* (these were blessed indeed); but he did not say anything related to *seeing God*. That is, Christ did *not* say, "Blessed are those who have not seen God and yet have believed in God" (it would not have contradicted the sixth beatitude, but he did not say so). What he said is this: "Blessed are those who have not seen [my Resurrection] and yet have believed [in it]." Certainly, those who believe in Christ Jesus' Resurrection even without seeing it are blessed in their attunement with their own resurrection through Christ. But believing in the Resurrection is not the same as seeing God. Therefore, for Christ, blessed are *both*: those who see God and those who (either seeing or not seeing God) believe in his Resurrection, and so in the Resurrection through Christ.

Other Christians do acknowledge that seeing God is important. However, they often think that seeing God means that they are to imagine God in what they see and in whom they meet. But Christ did *not* say that we are to imagine God in everything and everyone we encounter.[7] Such ways of thinking are not part of the Way of Christ—they make easy what is difficult, superficial what is profound. These ideas belong to naïve Christians, self-help teachers, or new-age prophets—those who seek to make their way to be the Way; it

---

6. Panikkar notices the connection between faith and various aspects revealed in seeing God (e.g., transcendence, infinitude, etc.): "Faith is a constitutive dimension of our being: an openness to the more, the unknown, transcendence, the infinite: openness to the given. Faith is an awareness that we are still on the way ... and, playing with words, the awareness that we are in-finite: *capax Dei*, the christian* tradition used to say, capable of receiving the Divine" (Panikkar, *Rhythm of Being*, 306) (*not capitalized in the original).

7. That by imagining God in others one will eventually see God (through some sort of actualized imagination) is more of a wish than a real possibility.

does not work. Seeing God implies attaining the perception of the Truth of being, beyond imagination. It is an outcome of the path that Christ laid down for us, which is challenging, transformative, and highly demanding (the road is narrow, so is the gate[8]). Therefore, the Christian needs to seek the real first and foremost, leaving imagination aside. Because the path that Christ laid down is based on truth and the direct experience of the real.

3. The Absolute

Jesus said, "Anyone who has seen me has seen the Father. How can you say, 'Show us the Father'?"

The testimony of those who have seen the Father is that of seeing the Absolute[9]—the omnipresent Truth, Consciousness, or true Self *in* all and *as* all. Those who see the Absolute realize the truth of the sixth beatitude— "The pure in heart . . . shall see God" (Matt 5:8 ESV). In their awareness, the space in between the objects of perception (e.g., between the objects displayed in a room, between one's self and the person one faces, between the veranda and the landscape) is not just colorless empty space but the active Being of God, a boundless ocean whose transparency does not preclude its apprehension. In such an awareness, one realizes the possibility of *peace*, as existential stability, inner quietude, and limitlessness. The Absolute is not an idea but a reality—it can be *seen*, as Jesus said, and *showed*, as Philip asked for.[10] That is: the Absolute exists as Ultimate Reality regardless of any idea of it being conceived and formulated, regardless of it being asserted or denied. Seeing the Absolute confirms the fact that the Living God is the real God. And seeing the real—the Absolute—is not a transitory vision of God; for temporary visions do not represent the uninterrupted apprehension of

---

8. Matt 7:13–14 (see both NIV and ESV); Luke 13:24.

9. The Absolute refers to the First Aspect of the Trinity—the Father. Here, "Aspect" means *hypostasis* (Greek). In like manner, Panikkar states: "In the christian* tradition this Absolute has a definite designation: 'The Father of our Lord Jesus Christ'. It is he indeed whom Jesus called his Father and God and also taught us to call our Father and God . . . The Father is the Absolute, the only God, *o theós*" (Panikkar, *Trinity*, 44) (*not capitalized in the original).

10. Panikkar states: "When the Christian discovers Christ in himself, when he lives the immanence to which he has been invited, he does not discover Jesus (Jesus is the mediator) but *he does see the Father* ("Philip, he who has seen me has seen the Father"), and becoming God, becomes everything. This kind of knowledge may be described as assimilation without loss of personal differentiation" (Panikkar, *Christophany*, 133; emphasis added).

reality—the Absolute, the Father, the Source. (They do not stand against it either. Indeed, in the Silence of being, the Absolute exists irrespective of any vision or temporary experience that we may have.)

We become aware of the Absolute through the sense of existence—the "I" sense—not through the senses; for the Absolute is not something with color and contour, texture and solidity, smell, taste, or sound which the senses can perceive. Even so, in order to realize the Absolute, there is no need to deny the senses, nor to negate the reality of their objects, as some Eastern paths propose.[11] We can simply access the Absolute through the colorless, surrounding, and always-available space that is necessary for everything else to be. Because space is Consciousness (i.e., it is empty of objects, but not of itself and of the awareness of itself), it relates to the existential "organ" of awareness of our being—the "I" sense—and so to the "I AM" of Christ. Hence, space opens our being to the "I AM" (Christ), who, being one with the Father, grants us (through our "I" sense) access to the Father—the Absolute. Yet further, the Absolute is not only accessible through the space in between objects, nor it is to be conceived as such (i.e., as "the in-between"), for all the objects we perceive are in space (i.e., *they do not push space away in order to be!*); in truth, everything *is* in space, just as everything *exists in* the Absolute, through Christ. Therefore, the Christian experience of God is not a negation of the world but the realization that *the world exists in God*, and further, that *the world is known by God*. Thus, the human being, by realizing the Absolute—the Father—bears witness *to* the world *of* the Source of its existence.

The way we make our awareness of the Absolute stable is by allowing the perception of the Absolute to be more obvious in our moments of rest: stopping the movements of attention to this-or-that and rejecting all "trying" and effort to see God, we can worship the God who *is* and who is revealed in contemplation—"*in* the Spirit and *in* truth" (John 4:24, emphasis added), as Christ said.[12] Such contemplative worship, not involving any imagination, causes the Absolute to be realized as the stable foundation of being. This is what the parable of the prodigal son[13] portrays: the *return* to the Father—the Source, the substratum of being and existence.[14] By allow-

---

11. See the expression *neti neti* (i.e., "not this, not that").
12. See chapter 6, section 3.
13. Luke 15:11–32.
14. Those who have realized the Absolute testify of their preceding path as a "path of *return*"; they feel as if they had been walking back to find their origin, the Source of

ing the perception of God to awaken in our consciousness, we are freed from egoistic desires and self-disturbing modes of deceitful imagination. Like the prodigal son who goes to the world to find his ruin in "wild living" (Luke 15:13) (so says the parable of Christ), we are lost until we find our way back to the Father; then we are embraced and "found" *in* the Father, and so we find ourselves in everything. As our existential attention is surrendered to the all-loving Father, God realization deepens in four stages: unlimited Space, all-pervading Consciousness, Emptiness, and undifferentiated Spirit.[15] But these stages still remind us of one same thing: that any imagination of God separates us from the awareness of the God who *is*—the Absolute, the Father, the Source of our being.

4. God Realization and the World

Jesus said, "Anyone who has seen me has seen the Father. How can you say, 'Show us the Father'?"

The kingdom of God is not an external reality to be looked at, as if coming from afar. Christ said, "The kingdom of God does not come with observation; nor will they say, 'See here!' or 'See there!'" (Luke 17:20–21 NKJV). Instead, the kingdom of God comes by realizing that God is omnipresent and that the light kingdom emerges within the interior of things, within the self, and in the world; just as Christ continued to say: "For indeed, the kingdom of God is within you" (17:21 NKJV). The kingdom "within you" involves the realization of God as the Heart within all that is, for God is realized in the self (i.e., with*in* "you") but cannot be contained in a limited self—he is omnipresent (i.e., present in all there is, both within and without). Indeed, God can be apprehended in all that the God-realized self can see. Such an experience can be amplified—enhanced by the Light revealed during individual or communal practice (that is what some Christians understand as the kingdom being "among us").[16] And

---

their existence. This Source is realized as the *substratum* of all, and in all, permanently. Panikkar reminds us of such a theological position, which agrees with mystical experience: "The Nicene Creed, as also the greek* Fathers and even Tertullian, affirms that the 'substratum' of the Divinity resides in the Father. It is only with Augustine that the Divinity as the substratum which imparts unity to the Trinity begins to be considered common to the three persons" (Panikkar, *Trinity*, 45) (*not capitalized in the original).

15. Portilla, *Spiritual Experience*, 234, 236–38.

16. The NIV reads, "The kingdom of God is in your midst" (Luke 17:21), which can be interpreted as the kingdom being located (or accessed) at the core of perception, but

there is a further experience—the descent of the Spirit—which does *not* mean that the kingdom of God is above us (as if it were removed from us) but that the realization of the kingdom within us (the experience of the Father, the Absolute) and among us (the experience of the Son, the Light) is sanctified by the Divine Spirit. For "the Spirit gives birth to spirit" (John 3:6), Jesus said.[17] And so, the Spirit descends, infusing Love (Agape) into God realization, and amplifying the experience of Christ—the Light. In doing so, the experience of the Divine appears complete (in being fulfilling to the soul and being).[18]

Without the realization of the Absolute, a Christian cannot gain existential peace. Hence, if Christians do not give importance to the realization of the Absolute, then the ways they interact with the world will not necessarily reflect the peace of God. Christians tend to be moral, reliable, comforting (Christian indeed); yet, rarely they are "profound" in their peace. There could be a formidable power in Christianity if it were to present itself, up front, acknowledging the experience of the Father—the Absolute. When taken as a common ground with other faiths, the Absolute opens the possibility of genuine existential dialogue,[19] presenting Christ's contribution to humanity departing from a shared experienced of peace. For, Christ brought the seed of Divine Life to Earth—a new teaching and a new way of relating to each other, in peace; "Peace I leave with you; my peace I give you" (John 14:27), he said. Yet, without the existential peace given by God realization, a Christian remains unaware of how lasting peace is conveyed and established in the world. Thus, God realization—seeing God through a pure heart (sixth beatitude)—is central to Christian life. It shall *never be downplayed*—it brings peace to the world in alignment with eternal life. While the experience of the Holy Spirit is commonly accepted as necessary

---

also in the middle of the faithful—through the conscious communion created by them.

17. See John 3:1–21. Here, we see that a condition for entering the kingdom of God is the Baptism of water and the Spirit (3:5–6). Through the Spirit, the Christian dies to the self and is born into Life; then God needs to be realized as the *substratum* of existence—the Father.

18. There is a sense of completeness in the experience of the Trinity, which attests to the reality and importance of such an understanding of God.

19. Such common ground may be a base for interreligious/interfaith dialogue (i.e., for the meeting of faith traditions with the purpose of mutual understanding, learning, and growth). See references in chapter 5, section 1. See the use of Ultimate Reality (i.e., the Absolute) in the "Points of Agreement" of the Snowmass Interreligious Conference, and also the commentaries by Thomas Keating and other participants, in Miles-Yepez, *Common Heart*, intro. and chap. 2 ("Opening a Dialogue").

How Can You Say, "Show Us the Father?"

for all Christians, to understand that God is the Trinity implies knowing the Father as well, and so the Son—the Light of being. Indeed, both the Son and the Father are coessential for Jesus, as he says: "Anyone who has seen me has seen the Father. How can you say, 'Show us the Father'?"

Even so, God realization is not to be imposed or hurried; the Christian must obtain maturity in the Way of Christ to gain the awareness of God with *stability and responsibility*. Further, God realization should never be considered an "extraordinary event" or an "altered state" (as psychology may put it). Christians are to think differently—nowadays, in a *countercultural* way—regarding the experience of God. God realization implies an awareness which embraces sensorial perceptions—what we see, touch, hear—in the ordinary activities of life; hence, it is an *ordinary awareness* that is sought for, not in the sense of being unimportant but as a perception integrated with all life. It is a matter between God and the soul, with the promise of a Divine Life. Yet, the current spiritual culture is not interested in Divine Life—it seeks temporary ecstasy, superficial relief, and wellness living, resulting in weak and often dualistic spirituality. God realization in the Christian Way is different, and interpreted differently: it is a matter of responsibility toward God and Christ. What we see through our plain sight does not preclude the realization of the Absolute—the Father. On the contrary: the world is apprehended through God realization in a different and truly inclusive way (i.e., there is a better order, and so a better ordinariness); but also, the world, in its limitation, reveals God as the Infinite—as the other side of the coin.[20] If God is omnipresent and also the foundation of Life, he cannot remove himself from Life. Hence, the Christian aspiration is not to leave the world[21] but to remain in the world, apprehending the

---

20. This idea resembles Max Müller's reflections on religion as the experience of the Infinite: "The reason why we cannot conceive an absolute limit is because we never perceive an absolute limit; or, in other words, because in perceiving the finite we always perceive the infinite also" (Müller, *Gifford Lectures*, 122–23). In a complementary way, Emmanuel Levinas states: "It is as though the psyche in subjectivity were equivalent to the negation* of the finite by the Infinite, as though—without wanting to play on words—the *in* of the Infinite were to signify both the *non* and the *within*." He continues: *"The latent birth of negation occurs not in subjectivity but in the idea of the Infinite. Or, if one prefers, it is in subjectivity qua idea of the Infinite. It is in this sense that the idea of the Infinite, as Descartes affirms, is a 'genuine idea' and not merely what I conceive 'by the negation of what is finite'" (Levinas, *Philosophical Writings*, 136, 189n11).

21. "My prayer is not that you take them out of the world but that you protect them from the evil one" (John 17:15).

world in God, and God in the world. (Such is Christian non-dual awareness, which avoids the dualism of transcendentalism.)

5. The Glory of the Transfiguration

Jesus said, "Anyone who has seen me has seen the Father. How can you say, 'Show us the Father'?"

Realizing the Father—the Absolute—is not the same as seeing the Glory of God. The Transfiguration of Christ Jesus is the event that makes the Glory of God manifest, when Jesus' face "shone like the sun, and his clothes became as white as the light" (Matt 17:2). The Transfiguration,[22] as witnessed by Peter, James, and John, occurs in the presence of Moses (representing the law) and Elijah (representing the prophets). The presence of Moses and Elijah in the Transfiguration shows that there is a relationship between the law, the prophets, and the Glory of God *in* Christ. Such a relationship is this: there was Grace in the law and the prophets, but now, the fullness of the Grace of God is revealed in Christ. The Gospel of John reads: "Out of his fullness we have all received grace in place of grace already given. For the law was given through Moses; grace and truth came through Jesus Christ" (John 1:16–17). Thus, there is a consummation of Grace with Christ Jesus; Light is revealed, making it obvious in the Transfiguration, when, through the Logos incarnate, the Glory of God is seen in the face of Christ.[23]

The presence of the apostles in the Transfiguration shows the association between Christ's Glory and those who are to convey such Glory to the world. Philip had not been present in the Transfiguration; yet, Jesus' answer—"Anyone who has seen me has seen the Father. How can you say, 'Show us the Father'?"—implies that Philip (and others) may have seen his Glory as well. The Gospel of John reads: "The Word became flesh and made his dwelling among us. *We have seen his glory*, the glory of the one and only Son, who came from the Father, full of grace and truth" (John 1:14, emphasis added). It is Christ—the Logos incarnate in the humanness of being, the embodied Light outshining corporality—whom the disciples should have seen. And it is this Light, manifesting itself in the I AM who Christ is, that

---

22. The Transfiguration is described in Matt 17:1–8; Mark 9:2–8; Luke 9:28–36.

23. "For God, who said, 'Let light shine out of darkness,' made *his light shine in our hearts* to give us *the light of the knowledge of God's glory* displayed in the face of Christ" (2 Cor 4:6, emphasis added).

prepares one to see the Father. Christ says: "If you really know me, you will know my Father as well. From now on, you do know him and have seen him" (John 14:7). Certainly, if by looking with faith to a godly person one receives their blessing (as a reflection of their being in one's own being),[24] so much more could be expected from seeing Christ Jesus, the Son of God, in his Glory. Christians, from the time of the apostles, are to be witnesses of God in the contemplation of the Father and in the Light manifested in the contemplation of each other—through Christ. For Jesus' statement "I am in the Father and the Father is in me" (John 14:11) is not only true for Christ but for others as well, just as Christ prayed: "I in them and you in me—so that they may be brought to complete unity" (John 17:23).

Christ is the Logos incarnate. The connection between the Light and the Life of sentient creation is revealed as the Light in the Son of Man. Through Christ Jesus, the powers of the Logos can manifest themselves and be apprehended by others—God becomes known to the Life of the human being. Thus, the transfiguration of the Christian in the Light is possible after Jesus' Transfiguration, for everything is possible in oneness with Christ.[25] Some may ask how seeing God as the Absolute and the experience of the Christ Light complement each other, because there is a difference between the permanent apprehension of the Absolute and the temporary transfiguration of our being in the Light. In this regard, the Gospels tell us we are endowed with various senses of perception to apprehend God. One is the heart—the epicenter of being, where the "I" sense, the soul, has its seat. Through the heart, we see God (sixth beatitude) as the Absolute. Another sense is the spiritual eye, which is activated by God, causing our temporary transfiguration in the Light. As Jesus said: "The eye is the lamp of the body. If your eyes are healthy, your whole body will be full of light" (Matt 6:22).[26] We participate in these events in the Glory of God, all the senses of divine perception being involved—heart, but also the soul; being,

---

24. In Hinduism, for example, the seeing of a godly person (*darshan*) implies a blessing in the form of a mutual recognition of divinity—an existential mechanism that is formalized as an important practice in this religion.

25. Similarly, Gregory Palamas states: "For it is in the glory of the Father that Christ will come again, and it is in the glory of their father,* Christ, that 'the just will shine like the sun'; they will be light, and will see the light, a sight delightful and all-holy, belonging only to the purified heart" (Palamas, *Triads*, 67). *The spiritual paternity of Christ is not unusual in patristic writers; Palamas's theology can be read as a conversation between patristic thinkers and Orthodox mysticism. See chapter 2, section 7, and the examples of transfiguration in the Light in the footnotes.

26. See also Luke 11:34.

as well as the eye. Thus, the path toward a fuller apprehension of God lies in the purification of the soul and heart and the regeneration of the connection between seeing and being.

6. "I AM"

Jesus said, "Anyone who has seen me has seen the Father. How can you say, 'Show us the Father'?"

The LORD revealed his Name to Moses; he later revealed himself *as* Jesus Christ. The LORD said to Moses, "I AM WHO I AM" (Exod 3:14 NKJV), disclosing also how he should be known—I AM; for this is how Moses was to address the children of Israel: "I AM has sent me [Moses] to you" (3:14 NKJV). Christ said who he is as well: I AM. He meant it in Eternity: "Before Abraham was, I AM" (John 8:58 NKJV). And it was demonstrated with power: at the garden of Gethsemane when he uttered, "I am He," those seeking to arrest him "fell to the ground" (John 18:6 NKJV).[27] The LORD revealed himself to Moses as a being in Holy Fire, appearing "from within the bush" (Exod 3:4); with Christ, the Holy Fire came at Pentecost, in Christ's Name. The LORD revealed himself to Moses as the almighty I AM; in Christ, as the I AM who is the Resurrection and the Life.[28] So the prayer of Jesus was fulfilled: "I made known to them your name, and I will continue to make it known, that the love with which you have loved me may be in them, and I in them" (John 17:26 ESV).[29]

Hence, the Living God reveals he is the I AM. But, who and what is the I AM? The I AM is the Trinity: the Universal Spirit, or omnipresent Absolute (THAT I AM, the Father); the Personal Spirit, or Light of being (WHO I AM, the Son); the dynamic Spirit Force (WHO I WILL BE, the Holy Spirit).[30] The I AM is also the triadic Being: the calm latency of Being

---

27. Also, in Acts, Paul recalls: "I saw a light from heaven, brighter than the sun, blazing around me and my companions. We all *fell to the ground*, and I heard a voice saying to me in Aramaic, 'Saul, Saul, why do you persecute me? It is hard for you to kick against the goads'" (26:13–14, emphasis added).

28. John 11:25.

29. See also: "I have manifested your name to the people whom you gave me out of the world. . . . keep them in your name, which you have given me, that they may be one, even as we are one . . . I kept them in your name" (John 17:6, 11, 12 ESV).

30. Most translations of the Name (or Who) of God in Exod 3:14 use WHO (NIV, ESV, NKJV). A trinitarian perspective, however, would welcome three complementary translations: I AM THAT I AM (Father), I AM WHO I AM (Son), I WILL BE WHO/

(experienced in the Father); the fullness of Being (experienced through the Son); Being that is also Becoming (experienced by the Spirit). And this is how the I AM is to be known—by following a *threefold practice* aligned with the triadic Being. That is: first, paying attention to the sense of existence (the "I" sense), which reveals the presence of the universal I AM—the Father; second, holding to the teachings of Christ (the Word) and receiving the Christian Initiations, which reveal the Son as the Light and Life; third, surrendering to the workings of the Spirit—God's dynamic will—thus accepting the Open Gospel, in which the destiny of human life is cocreated in the awareness of God.[31]

In Christ, all the geometries and mathematics of Living Light abiding within the Logos are manifested into being. The Father—THAT I AM—comes into being through the Son—WHO I AM. Because of the identity of the Son with human life (through the Incarnation, Atonement, Resurrection, and the coming of the Fire of Life at Pentecost), the human being is no longer removed from Life. Through Christ, the human being can aspire to be more than just a pale reflection of the Logos, becoming one with the potentiality residing in WHO I AM. Divine Life on Earth became a real possibility through Christ, once the I AM incarnated in Jesus as a human "who." By abiding in WHO I AM (Christ), we make our being participant of the Light employed in our genesis; in doing so, we become cocreators of the Divine Life to come. We may then experience Divine Love, which is no different from God's will (WHO I WILL BE) acting through the Logos (WHO I AM) within the primordial reality of Being (THAT I AM).

7. Knowing God Fully

Jesus said, "Anyone who has seen me has seen the Father. How can you say, 'Show us the Father'?"

The Gospel of John reads: "No one has ever seen God, but the one and only Son, who is himself God and is in *closest relationship* with the Father, has made him known" (John 1:18, emphasis added). It is not that God was not known before the Incarnation of Christ; certainly, God, as the Absolute, was known to the ancient sages.[32] Yet also, the Logos is present in creation

---

THAT I WILL BE (Spirit).

31. John 14:26. See also John 14:12. The Open Gospel implies a continuous "good news" and a renewal and broadening of the "good news" through the Spirit.

32. Seeing God as the Universal Spirit, the Self, or all-pervading Consciousness was a

and so in the consciousness of the human being from the start: "He was with God in the beginning. Through him all things were made; without him nothing was made that has been made. In him was life, and that life was the light of all mankind" (John 1:2-4). And so, God could be known through the Logos—WHO I AM—even before the Logos made himself known in Jesus Christ; as Christ said, "Before Abraham was, I AM" (John 8:58 NKJV). Even so, the Glory of God—the fullness of the Light of the Living God—was revealed to humanity in Christ, the Son, "who is himself God and is in *closest relationship* with the Father" (John 1:18, emphasis added).[33] Thus, the uniqueness of Christianity is not found in the perception of the Father as the Absolute but in the apprehension of the Glory of the Father through the Son. Christ Jesus demonstrated that he was closest to the Father not because he saw the Father but because of his *unique apprehension* of the Father: first, he embodied the realization of God in a unparalleled, caring, humane way; second, his body was transfigured in Light; third, he was resurrected from the dead, thus demonstrating the deepest possible apprehension of God—the bodily apprehension. (Indeed, sentient Matter was included in *conscious* Divine Existence through the Son.)

Hence, Christ Jesus' saying, "No one comes to the Father except through me. If you really know me, you will know my Father as well. From now on, you do know him and have seen him" (John 14:6-7), is not a negation of other faiths—of their truths and ways to know God—but an assertion of Christ's presence, as primordial Logos, I AM, in all those who know God.[34] Yet further, only because the Logos incarnated and was enthroned in sentient Matter (through the Resurrection) may we come to know the Father fully—with all aspects of our being. And so, what Christians are to attain through Christ is not only the soul apprehension of the Absolute (the

---

type of perception already known to the ancient sages in India hundreds of years before Christ. They also knew how to touch the Light above by raising their consciousness over earthly existence and how to grant Liberation to their souls (*moksha, mukti*).

33. The Gospel does *not* say the *only* relationship, but the "closest."

34. For example, Augustine, before his conversion to Christianity, seems to have had an experience of the Absolute following the Platonic school (even in an unstable manner): "For unless, by some means, it had known the immutable, it could not possibly have been certain that it was preferable to the mutable. And so, in an instant of awe, my mind attained to the sight of the God who IS. Then, at last, *I caught sight of your invisible nature, as it is known through your creatures*. But I had no strength to fix my gaze upon them. In my weakness I recoiled and fell back into my old ways, carrying with me nothing but the memory of something that I loved and longed for, as though I had sensed the fragrance of the fare but was not yet able to eat it" (Augustine, *Confessions*, 151-52).

Father) but a full participation in the Absolute, including all aspects of being (even the body). And such embodied divinity is to be brought forth in social relations *in* Christ. Because to have the aspiration to know the Father *fully* implies that we are to acknowledge ourselves and any other person not just as a divine soul but as a divine being completely; hence, we should respect the physicality of others, just as we ought to respect our own. Such an all-inclusive way of acknowledging ourselves and any other person is the unique christening perception given by Christ to us.

In sum: the ancient sages knew of the possibility of union between the soul (the "I" sense) and the transcendent Spirit,[35] and so they knew how to acknowledge all sentient beings in the truth of God; yet the divine inclusion of physicality was absent.[36] Through Christ's Sacrifice, our conditions changed: the Light came to stay; the doors to the Divine were opened for its descent; the Fire of Regeneration was sent for the glorification of our being. It is the perception of the Trinity, inclusive of all aspects of being, and the Love that comes with it—toward our fellow human beings—that Christ made available to us. And because of the all-inclusive character of Christ's Love, the Christian impulse is to transform human existence (not just to transcend it, as the ancient sages were certainly capable of). Such Love challenges what is hidden in us and in those with whom we interact, because nothing of our humanity is left apart from the Living God (the basis of our genesis). Embracing this inclusive way, which brings all that we encounter to the Light, we come to know the Father more profoundly—in ourselves and in others—through Christ.

---

35. In Christian mysticism, we can also find this ancient perspective and its transcendent experience; Teresa of Ávila (i.e., Teresa de Jesús), regarding the experience of the body upon the soul's union with God (the Absolute, the Universal Spirit), states: "I have already said that . . . here [at this seventh stage] there is no memory of the body . . . but only Spirit, and in the spiritual matrimony much less, because this secret union happens in the very interior center of the soul, which must be where God himself is and, it seems to me, there is no (need of) a door from where he enters" (Teresa de Jesús, *Las moradas*, 213 [Seventh Abode 2:3], my translation). Spanish original: "Ya he dicho que . . . aquí no hay memoria de cuerpo . . . sino sólo espíritu, y en el matrimonio espiritual muy menos, porque pasa esta secreta unión en el centro muy interior del alma, que debe ser adonde está el mismo Dios y, a mi parecer, no ha menester puerta por donde entre."

36. They pursued paths of individual Liberation, mostly in isolation, because such was the highest spiritual aspiration possible in those times—not because they wanted it to be so but because it was so before Christ.

Truth

To pursue the Christian path involves facilitating the expression of the Trinity through our individual and collective being. Living Christ's teachings involves both inquiry and practice, together with the experience of God. To see the Father—the Absolute—is not to be forgotten, for seeing the Father is necessary in order to obtain the christening perception of others and the world. Jesus assumed that those following his Way would come to see the Father while living and as *a matter of course*. He said to Philip: "Anyone who has seen me has seen the Father. How can you say, 'Show us the Father'?" Thus, Christians are to consider seeing the Father as an important stepping-stone in the Way of Christ.

CHAPTER 10

I Will Not Leave You as Orphans
The Immanent Truth of Christ

1. The Christ Remained

JESUS SAID, "I WILL not leave you as orphans; I will come to you" (John 14:18).

Christians start their journey by becoming "children of God" (John 1:12).[1] To become children—spiritually—does not imply a return to one's own childhood;[2] it is rather a new birth—through the Spirit—leading to spiritual adulthood as we become more conscious of God. Indeed, Christ loves us as children at first;[3] yet, this relationship matures into

---

1. "Yet to all who did receive him, to those who believed in his name, he gave the right to become children of God—*children born not of natural descent, nor of human decision* or a husband's will, but born of God" (John 1:12–13, emphasis added). Paul states: "I could not address you as people who live by the Spirit but as people who are *still worldly—mere infants in Christ*. I gave you *milk, not solid food*, for you were not yet ready for it. Indeed, you are still not ready" (1 Cor 3:1–2, emphasis added).

2. Paul continues: "Brothers and sisters, stop thinking like children. In regard to evil be infants, but *in your thinking be adults*" (1 Cor 14:20, emphasis added). This follows what Jesus said in Matt 10:16: "Be wise as serpents and innocent as doves" (ESV). Mark 10:15, Luke 18:17, and Matt 19:14 are to be read differentiating childlike heart availability in relation to God and the kingdom from idealized states of ignorance and infantile behavior. Certainly, *Christ never behaved as if he were a child or lacking adult reason*—his words and actions came out of godly wisdom and higher-reasoning principles.

3. The disciples are not left "as orphans"; this expression suggests that Christ is accepting a parental role. Patristic writers recognized the paternity of Christ: "For it is in

our "fellowship" with him and the Father (1 John 1:3)—just as he eventually said to his disciples: "I have called you friends, for everything that I learned from my Father I have made known to you" (John 15:15).[4] But also, having shared much with his disciples—awakened them to a new vision of Life—Christ remained with them; that is: he did not leave them "as orphans" after calling them "friends." "I will come to you," he said; for their fellowship was to continue. He promised them that the Fire of Life—the Holy Spirit—would come in his Name (and it came). He promised them that he would manifest himself and come to them (and he did).[5] He said after his Resurrection: "I am with you always, to the very end of the age" (Matt 28:20). Hence, as it had been "heard from the Law" (John 12:34), the Christ *remained*.[6]

2. A Culture of Becoming

Jesus said, "I will not leave you as orphans; I will come to you."

Our present culture is a culture of becoming—not of *being*. There is a constant urge to always seek for "the next"—level, thing, or experience—often losing sight of what is given in the "now." Rarely is a person courageous enough to stop, for a period awkward to the onlooker, and to appreciate what life offers by *just being*. Christians are not wiser in this respect than any other person: they think that it is fine to be always looking forward, not realizing how much a culture of becoming limits their understanding of Christ. A culture of becoming makes the Christian think constantly about

---

the glory of the Father that Christ will come again, and it is *in the glory of their father, Christ*, that 'the just will shine like the sun'" (Palamas, *Triads*, 67, 136n80, 133n38); emphasis added). It is common for spiritual masters to see their disciples as "spiritual children" until they reach maturity in God. Certainly, it is difficult to conceive a mature relationship with Christ—friendship and fellowship—without due discipleship first. Hebrews 2:11-13 suggests the possibility of developing overlapping relationships with Jesus as both brother and parent (in a spiritual sense, of course). See chapter 4, section 5.

4. Here, "friends" is a development from "servants": "I no longer call you servants, because a servant does not know his master's business" (John 15:15); probably, Jesus is advancing the forthcoming change of their status from disciples that just follow (him and his teachings) to disciples who would have to develop the teachings through the Spirit, in fellowship with him and the Father.

5. John 14:21, 18, NKJV.

6. See John 12:34-36. Christ remained, manifesting himself in various ways: as the inherent Light of being; as the Moral Being (the power that overcomes sin); as the Logos in Christ Events or Pauline Events.

the Christ who will come, not about the Christ who *is* and who is found in Being. In a *countercultural* way, the Christian must be grounded in Being, even if not in a static way. The Son is of the Father (Being), while the Spirit (Becoming) is sent by the Father and the Son in Christ's Name. Therefore, Becoming is always grounded in Being through Christ (the Son of Being). Consequently, we do not live in the intersection of Being and Becoming; rather, we live *as in* Being, from which Becoming, as Love, comes forth. And we live in the harmony of Being because of the Son, who is the coherent Logos, the Light, the Word. Thus, Christians should not accommodate to a culture of becoming but remain grounded in Being, while reflecting the dynamism of the Trinity by *just being*.

The living understanding of Christ should include both: an immanent Christ—the Light of being established through the Office of Christ, a Christ Light which never left—and a later coming, which points toward a Divine Life and a resurrected Matter, a different way of apprehending existence and of understanding creation that is free from the restrictions of linear time. That is, the immanent Christ *is* always and everywhere, just as God—as immanent reality—*is*; for an omnipresent God cannot *not* be or stop being all-pervading and therefore immanent. And so, Christ—"who is himself God" (John 1:18)—must be immanent, as God. Further, Christ is accessible within the *humanness of being*, for he incarnated as a human being, showing to others his Glory[7] and attaining Resurrection, which is the seed of Divine Life in the New Earth. Even so, as far as we do not experience a fulfilling Divine Life, there will be some expectation—the hope for a more satisfying future.[8]

Thus, Christians are to live with the *certainty* of the immanent Christ—the Christ Light manifesting itself in being—while accepting the *wonderment* of the coming. The way to existentially conciliate the two is by understanding that the Resurrection occurs in Eternity and that our present moment is happening in Eternity. That is: it is by embodying Eternity and

---

7. John 1:14.

8. It is for this reason that, as N. T. Wright explains, "early Christians developed a 'now-and-not-yet' approach." Wright continues: "Something *had happened* as a result of which the expected kingdom was, in one sense, a present reality, and something *was yet to happen* through which that already-inaugurated kingdom would reach its ultimate goal"; "Jesus is already 'crowned with glory and honor,' but there will be a fuller sovereignty, for the whole redeemed human race, yet to come"; "The eschatology is a long way from being 'realized.' But it has been well and truly inaugurated" (Wright, "Hope Deferred?" 57, 68, 74). See also the general critique of "the Dogma of Delay" in this article.

letting go of linear time as the main lens through which one looks to divine events that the Christian participates in the mysteries of God as revealed through Jesus Christ. Thus, the Christian is to participate in the Christ Light manifesting itself in a present that gives testimony of a hoped-for bright future. Some Christians think of the coming of Christ as an external event disconnected from their present lives (the saying "Why do you stand here looking into the sky?" [Acts 1:11] applies to them);[9] they understand neither the immanent Christ nor that the nature of Christ's coming implies the transformation of the Earth while being always connected to a present reality that lives in Eternity. Any form of Christianity which remains grounded in Being, thus resisting the culture of becoming, would be less limited in its understanding of Christ.

3. The Immanent Christ

Jesus said, "I will not leave you as orphans; I will come to you."

Before his arrest and trial, Christ tells his disciples that they will soon experience three interrelated events.[10] First, the Father will send the Spirit in his Name—the Fire of Life—to be *with* them and *in* them forever.[11] Second, he will come to them and show himself, and they will see him (as happened to Paul on the road to Damascus, for example).[12] Third, they will realize that Christ is in the Father, that they are in Christ, and that Christ is in them; that is, they will see that the Light is in the Absolute, that their being rests in the Light, and that ultimately, the Light can manifest itself in and through them.[13] In sum: Christ Jesus promises his disciples that they

---

9. So said the "two men dressed in white" (Acts 1:10).

10. John 14:15–21. All three experiential events are mentioned in this short passage.

11. John 14:15–17. The Christian Initiation of the Holy Spirit as the Fire of Life is different from the Baptism of the Holy Spirit as a Force or Power. When Christ foretold the Baptism of Fire, the Baptism of the Spirit Force had already been given to many—by both Christ (after the Spirit Force descended on him in the river Jordan) and his disciples (after being empowered by him); see John 3:22–26; 4:1–2; 7:38–39. Both Baptisms—Force (first) *and* Fire (later)—were foretold by John the Baptist in his role as the precursor of Christ (Matt 3:11; Luke 3:16). The Holy Spirit, understood as the Fire of Life, is sent in Christ's Name (John 14:26).

12. John 14:18–19, 21. Here, it seems that Christ is referring to a way of seeing him that is different from beholding the resurrected Christ; a way that will remain possible after his physical departure: "Before long, the world will not see me anymore, but you will see me. Because I live, you also will live" (14:19).

13. John 14:20.

are to enter into communion with the Father, himself, and the Fire of Life as a living realization then and forever. All these interrelated experiences represent the realization of the immanent Christ. They have been testified about by Christians throughout history, thus becoming facts of Christian existence and part of the Open Gospel of Christ.[14]

Through the three interrelated events, the Father and Christ—the Absolute and the Light—become the true home of the Christian who observes Christ's teaching. Jesus said: "Anyone who loves me will obey my teaching. My Father will love them, and we will come to them and make our home with them" (John 14:23). Thus, loving Christ is central to following his teaching, for Christian discipleship comes out of love. But loving Christ is also necessary to see Christ (the Light); indeed, the apostle Jude was asking Christ on this occasion the reason why he would show himself to them and not to the world, and Christ replied that it is precisely because of the lack of love.[15] Hence, even if Christ is immanent—existing in all—he is revealed to a person because of their love for him, and so because of their discipleship. This is evident in the way Jesus had begun this conversation: "Whoever has my commands and keeps them is the one who loves me. The one who loves me will be loved by my Father, and I too will love them and show myself to them" (John 14:21). The true home of existence is thus found by knowing the immanent Christ and the Father, who are one.[16] If so, Christians who do not meet the requirements for knowing Christ and the Father may find themselves "homeless"—seeking an extraneous light which is not the immanent Christ Light living within their being.

Realizing the immanent Christ shows that the reality of God is that of the omnipresent "here." Recognizing that there is a Divine above is not in conflict with the testimony of God as being immanent. A Divine above agrees with the experience of Spiritual Baptism, with the ups and downs of the Spirit—the processes of ascent of consciousness and of descent of the Force, resulting in Agape (Divine Love) engulfing one's own being. These experiences complement those of the Father (the Absolute, the horizon of being) and of the Son (the Light, the glow of being); further, such vertical experiences (of ascent and descent) are different from mere ideas of God

---

14. As explained in chapter 9, the Open Gospel implies a continuation of the "good news"—the renewal and broadening of the "good news" through the Spirit, not confined to the narratives of the New Testament.

15. John 14:21–24.

16. Coessential.

being just above, which may refer to some heavenly realm but not to what God is—Spirit, Light, and Love.[17] The immanent Christ harmonizes us and roots the Spirit coming from above in the "here"—in *being*—for the Power of God cannot be in us without Christ, who gives us peace and stability. Indeed, Christ Jesus did not physically depart without giving such comfort: "Peace I leave with you; my peace I give you" (John 14:27), he said.[18] The immanent Christ is omnipresent, a fact of the "here," and never apart from *being*.

4. The Coming of the "Son of Man"

Jesus said, "I will not leave you as orphans; I will come to you."

The image of God is the Absolute; the similitude is form in alignment with the Absolute (expressing God's likeness).[19] "Man"—the human being—was created in the image and similitude of God and is destined to become conscious of such a condition. The Son of "Man" is the inherent image and similitude in the Eternal Christ—the Logos—in whose Name lies the Fire of Life, waiting to be sent to Earth, for whatever it engulfs becomes one with eternal life.[20] God makes the human being in his image and similitude (Adam and Eve, man and woman), but that human being is not like the Son of Man.[21] The Eternal Christ manifests himself to Moses as a being engulfed in Holy Fire (a Fire which does not burn because it is the Fire of Life).[22] On that occasion, the Eternal Christ reveals who the

---

17. John 4:24; 1 John 1:5; 1 John 4:16.

18. This saying is uttered before the Passion and Resurrection. The resurrected Christ also gave peace (John 20:19, 21, 26).

19. Recovering the similitude (or likeness) is associated with the *embodied* Light of being. The Hebrew word for "likeness" also means "form" (see Ps 17:15).

20. See the following expressions: "came down" (John 3:13 NKJV); "ascend to where he was before!" (6:62 NIV); "I came from the Father" (16:28 NIV). See also Dan 7:13. The Father and Christ send the Fire of Life in Christ's Name (John 14:26; 16:7).

21. The human being became "like" God (Elohim) once they knew good and evil; eating from the tree of life was postponed so that the human being would not "live forever" (Gen 3:22). See chapter 2, section 3.

22. Exod 3:2–3, 6, 14. This reading is not new: "The Angel (or Messenger) of the Lord who appeared to Moses and spoke with 'the voice of the Lord' (v. 31) is the *eternal Christ*, according to the interpretation of the Church Fathers. Christ is the agent of creation and revelation (John 1:1–4), and thus was already active in the OT in a hidden way" (Gillquist, *Orthodox Study Bible*, 286; emphasis added, boldface removed). This event is also mentioned in Acts 7:30, Mark 12:26, and Luke 20:37. In Mark and Luke, the word

Lord is—I AM WHO I AM—but does not stay on Earth: it is not a human incarnation; it is not yet the coming of the Son of Man to Earth. (These were the conditions before the Incarnation of Christ.)

Christ Jesus is the coming of the Son of Man as Messiah—the Son of the Living God. Christ Jesus calls himself "Son of Man" because he knows who he is, and he knows his mission.[23] His disciples think of him both as a teacher (rabbi) and as the Son of God; but they do not know the full extent of Christ's nature and Office. Indeed, while living with Christ, the disciples did not expect the Atonement, the Resurrection, and the coming of the Fire of Life at Pentecost: they did not know the importance of Christ Jesus as the Son of Man. The Son of Man—the inherent image and similitude in the

---

"burning" has been added in some translations, but it is *not used* in the Greek version (i.e., there is only reference to the "bush" (*batou, batos*), *not* to a "burning bush"). In Acts, the angel appears "in a flame of fire" (*en phlogi pyros*). That is, we should understand (and emphasize) that *the Fire of Life does not burn, for it is Life and gives Life*. The association between the Fire of Life, the Living God, the Logos (i.e., the Word, the Christ), and the higher divine beings is a fundamental one in Divine Reality. Dionysius the Areopagite states: "Those with a knowledge of Hebrew are aware of the fact that the holy name 'seraphim' means 'fire-makers,' that is to say, 'carriers of warmth' ... In general, whether the reference be to high or low within the hierarchy, the Word of God always honors the representation of fire. And indeed it seems to me that this imagery of fire best expresses the way in which the intelligent beings of heaven are like the Deity" (Dionysius the Areopagite, *Complete Works*, 161, 183). Likewise, the Hekhalot literature reads: "The cherubim of Your cherubim are fire, O One who is declared majestic over the cherubim of fire, [Seraphim are] seraphim of flame, surrounding [Your throne] they stand, each makes the other hear" (Davila, *Hekhalot Literature*, 385; corner brackets removed).

23. Jesus seems to have contextualized his understanding of the Son of Man, the coming kingdom, and his mission using recognizable scriptural passages. N. T. Wright states: "Each of these passages [Dan 7; Isa 52–3; Zech 9–14; Pss 93; 97; etc.] was about the coming of the kingdom. Each of them was about the radical defeat of the powers of evil. Each of them, obviously, was about the vindication of Israel, and/or her representative. Each of them, despite popular impressions to the contrary, could be read in the first century as being about a messianic figure or figures. Since we have already argued that these constituted the major elements of Jesus' kingdom-announcement, *there is every reason to suppose that he would have felt free to draw on these texts, in his own way*, as passages which in any case stood in the shadows behind the Maccabaean and other traditions that formed his more immediate context"; "Daniel, Zechariah and the Psalms thus contribute to various elements of Jesus' mindset, his *awareness of vocation*. The kingdom would come through the suffering of the righteous; the true king would share the suffering of the people ... But there is, as we have seen, one book which ... adds to them a stone which the builders regularly reject ... the claim that the redemption of Israel from exile and the suffering of the messianic figure, are linked precisely as effect and cause. I refer, of course, to Isaiah 40—55" (Wright, *Victory of God*, 598, 601; emphasis added [see 597–604, entire passage]). See also John 5:39, 46–47.

Eternal Christ, the Logos—becomes a human being (incarnates) to redeem the human condition and to bring it not to a prior Adamic and Evaic state but to a *Christ-like order of being*.

Through the Atonement and the Resurrection of the incarnated Son of Man, the seed of the resurrected New "Man"—a human being capable of abiding in the Glory of the Living God—is established on Earth. Yet, the Office of Christ is not finished with the Resurrection: the Son of Man, having apprehended all aspects of his humanity, including his physical body, must come back to the Father for the Fire of Life to come. And the Fire of Life must come (in Christ's Name) so that humanity may abide in the Eternal Christ—I AM WHO I AM (as revealed to Moses). That is: the Fire of Life must reach and engulf human reality, which now has become atoned by the Son of Man, so that the seed of the resurrected New "Man" may grow; so that the human being may become one with Life. Thus, the primordial association between the Fire of Life and God is fulfilled in the human being.[24] Human beings are then given the possibility of becoming conscious of being created in the image and similitude of God. (This is the meaning of the "Son of Man.")

5. Back to the Father—the Mechanics of Exchange

Jesus said, "I will not leave you as orphans; I will come to you."

Christ did not leave. It was his promise that he would remain—Christians would not be left as orphans. We know that this is true, for Christ can be perceived and known after his departure from the physical plane. Yet, some may ask: Why must the Son of Man go back to the Father and not simply stay in his resurrected condition on Earth? Indeed: Christ Jesus says explicitly that he must go; otherwise, the Fire of Life cannot come.[25] However, he does not explain why the Fire of Life cannot come if he remains physically. But this we should accept: Christ does not give reasons—he simply describes a *mechanics of exchange*; it is not the why but *the how* that is important for Christ to convey. The Son of Man must go

---

24. "O Lord my God, You are very great: . . . Who makes His angels spirits, His ministers a flame of fire. . . . You send forth Your Spirit, they are created; and You renew the face of the earth" (Ps 104:1, 4, 30 NKJV). Psalm 104 is sung at Pentecost. See also Heb 1:7.

25. "But very truly I tell you, it is for your good that I am going away. *Unless I go away*, the Advocate *will not come to you*; but if I go, *I will send him to you*" (John 16:7, emphasis added).

back to the Father so that he and the Father can send the Fire of Life in his Name.[26] It is not an option; it is not a good idea—it is *what is necessary* and *how it happens*.

Hence: the coming of the Holy Spirit—the Fire of Life—is necessary to finish the Office of Christ, but before this happens, Christ must physically go away. The resurrected human nature of Christ Jesus, one with the Son of Man, returns to the original indwelling place[27] of the Son of Man—the Eternal Christ—where the Fire of Life resides and awaits. Upon his return, there is a *mechanics of exchange*: the returned Christ Jesus, one with the Son of Man,[28] gives testimony of the resurrected human nature to the Father, now carrying with him the seed of the resurrected New "Man"—the human being capable of abiding in the Glory of the Living God. Then, there is a response: sent by the Father and Son, the Fire of Life comes and embraces human nature on Earth, making it part of its original realm. The human being is thus no longer separated from the fullness of the Eternal Christ, the LORD—I AM WHO I AM. From then on, the image and similitude of God, through the Fire of Life, become consciously accessible in the human condition.[29]

The *mechanics of exchange* reflects certain laws of God as well as of nature: for a seed to grow, it needs to "return" to the soil, the fertile ground;

26. John 16:28; see also 3:13; 6:62. Christ said: "Everyone will be salted with fire" (Mark 9:49). Although this passage has other interpretations, in this inquiry I suggest a mystical reading: the importance of acquiring *saltiness* by the Baptism of Fire. Moreover, seemingly foreseeing the Baptism of Fire, Christ said: "I have come to bring fire on the earth [the Baptism of Fire], and *how I wish it were already kindled*! But I have a baptism to undergo [the Passion], and what *constraint I am under until it is completed*!" (Luke 12:49–50, emphasis added). See also John 14:26 and Acts 1:3–8.

27. "My Father's house has many rooms; . . . And if I go and prepare a place for you, I will come back and take you to be with me that you also may be where I am. . . . You heard me say, 'I am going away and I am coming back to you.' If you loved me, you would be glad that I am going to the Father, for the Father is greater than I" (John 14:2–3; 14:28).

28. See passages related to the reception of the Son of Man into heaven (Mark 16:19; Luke 24:51; Acts 1:9; John 6:62). See also John 17:4–11.

29. We may note that in Jewish Merkavah mysticism, the practitioner's aim was to be temporarily transformed into "a being of fire; to join in the angelic liturgy in the divine throne room" (Davila, *Hekhalot Literature*, 1). Psalm 104:3–4 reads: "He makes the clouds his chariot and rides on the wings of the wind. He makes winds his messengers, flames of fire his servants." If the angelic liturgy was only available to Jewish mystics (i.e., highly advanced adepts with great spiritual capacity), we may tentatively see the sending of the Fire of Life "on all flesh" (Acts 2:16–17 NKJV), starting with the first Pentecostal Baptism, as making divine liturgy in Christ's Name available to the many, and without the need of departing from the Earth's physical realm.

likewise, for the New "Man" to grow, its seed must return to the Source, the Father, the foundation of Life. Thus, the resurrected Son of Man needs to go back to the Father for the Office of Christ to be completed—so that the seed of the resurrected New "Man" may grow and give fruit. Christians may think differently: some reason that the Father took back the Son of Man so that human beings would not depend on Jesus and would learn by themselves; others believe that since the Spirit "will teach ... all things" (John 14:26), then Jesus is not necessary. But Christ did not speak in those terms; he did not say he had to go away so that his disciples could learn without his help, nor that he would be unnecessary when the Spirit came. No; he said he had to go away for the Fire of Life to come (no didactical reasons for it). Even so, that going away only refers to the physical Incarnation—both the coming of the Son of Man and his kingdom have been *active from the beginning* of Christianity through the Fire of Life sent in Christ's Name (just as Christ Jesus said).[30] And so, any future coming is already operating after the *mechanics of exchange* took place. If Christians live with the expectation of a future coming which is disconnected with the present, they are limiting their experience of Christ; for the Office of Christ established the possibility of communion with Christ and of living in Eternity, then and forever.

6. The Immanent Life in Matter

Jesus said, "I will not leave you as orphans; I will come to you."

As a result of the Atonement, the Resurrection, and the coming of the Fire of Life, the human body is transfigured into a Life-bearing aspect of being. From then on, the human being must engage in an emerging Divine Existence. What makes it possible for us to hope for a New Earth, a better future, and a true Divine Life is the Resurrection; it is the event that makes the human body divine and not simply a vehicle for spiritual growth, as the paths before Christ understood it.[31] Hence, Christianity is based upon the contemplation of the Resurrection as an indwelling reality, which facilitates the possibility of abiding in the Light that Christ is in a way that includes

---

30. Matt 10:23; 16:28.

31. The spiritual paths of the East have often considered the physical body either as a "vehicle" for spiritual practice or as an irrelevant (at times problematic) aspect of being. That is, the bodily circumstance is mostly understood as *suffering*—an inconvenience—and so the adept or practitioner must strive to be free from it (by attaining Liberation or transcendence in one way or another).

our physicality. Yet, there is a tension between physicality and Light, which shows to what extent the personal self is still too concentrated on itself and not released into being. Such an untuned tension between sentient Matter and Spirit reflects other fundamental tensions as well: temporality and Eternity; the world and the Divine. It is the tension of the nature of things that cannot be fine-tuned without the realization of the immanent Christ and his conscious presence in sentient Matter; for the awareness of the immanent Christ is what releases the sense of finite self into the Infinite without the loss of personhood (as one is established in the personal I AM that Christ is).

The inward acceptance of Christ Jesus' resurrected body as a reality to be lived implies an unrelenting challenge to degenerative entropy: the ordinary conceptions of time and death are existentially questioned by the Christian through an increase of coherence and luminosity of being.[32] If Christ Jesus' Resurrection is the first fruit of the possibility of divinization of sentient Matter and the demonstration of the involvement of God's Love in material creation (so that creation can consciously participate in Eternity), then to experience and live such Love in human existence must be accepted as an essential aspiration for the Christian. Jesus said: "I am the resurrection and the life. The one who believes in me will live, even though they die; and whoever lives by believing in me will never die" (John 11:25–26). Therefore, by believing in Christ—in his Resurrection—our being lives in Eternity. If so, the major question regarding the Resurrection for a Christian is not whether they will be part of it after death but whether their being is consciously participating in Christ's Resurrection already—while living. Such being the case, the Christian would be living in Eternity—an Eternity in which life is not the opposite of death; for Eternity is an *existential continuum* in which Love is the underlying paradigm and "death," as we know it, is no more.

Thus, to accept Christ Jesus' Resurrection means accepting the possibility of relating to Life and worldly existence in a way that honors what the Logos is. The Logos is Light, and it is created Matter; from the moment the human body was resurrected in Christ Jesus, there could not be doubt

---

32. Internal *coherence* (of being) implies *correlation and dialogue between the constituents of being*. It follows Luke 11:35–36 in that the less inner darkness (i.e., confusion, degenerative tendencies, etc.—in sum, the fewer obstructions), the more inner coherence and luminosity. The terms "coherence" and "entropy" are mostly used in the fields of physics and biology; in this hermeneutical inquiry, they are contextually applied to the domain of Christian experience.

of the divine nature of sentient Matter and of the possibility of divine consciousness manifesting itself through it. Hence, if the Way of Christ calls for the Christian to live in Christ, then to live in Christ must be bodily inclusive—embracing the entire human condition. Christ Jesus provided us with the same Glory he received. He said to the Father: "I have given them the glory that you gave me" (John 17:22–23). And by that Glory we shall abide in harmony with the Father (the Absolute, the ground of being) and with Christ (the Life, the Light of being). The genuine and sincere aspiration toward embodied, Christ-like Love makes a Christian participant, to the extent that they are capable, of the Love of God for material creation in the way Christ made it possible.

7. Fruit of Living Fire

Jesus said, "I will not leave you as orphans; I will come to you."

In the Resurrection, Jesus' body is apprehended by the Divine in such a way that decay is not the necessary destiny of sentient Matter anymore: the Son of Man becomes one with the human condition as Life enters death, because the Son has "life in himself" (John 5:26).[33] What Christ Jesus is after his departure from the physical plane we know through the manifestation of the Light of being within us (among us, when we gather together) and because of the manifestations of his form in the Light which he is; these are experiential facts of Christian existence from the times of the apostles and Paul's encounter with Christ on the road to Damascus. However, what Christ Jesus physically is we cannot know but through inferences: by what Christ Jesus' Resurrection means in our Christian practice and how it informs our embodied experience of the Divine.[34]

The coming of the Fire of Life—the Pentecostal Spirit—activated the immanent Christ in human existence. Christians are thus given the opportunity to participate in the divine formation of what the human *is* and *is to be* in a renewed Earth as the consciousness of the image and similitude of God awakens in them. Such an opportunity was given through a two-step process: first, the Logos incarnated in a human body for the sake of all human "others"; second, the Fire of Life—the Advocate sent by the Father

---

33. See John 1:4; 5:26–27.

34. Only through experiential, corporeal means—by experiencing the Divine in sentient Matter—we may know (or hint at) what Christ Jesus is in the Resurrection and how such a state interacts with human existence.

and Son in Christ's Name—activated the immanent Christ (the I AM that Christ is) in those who received it. From then on, Christianity becomes a living and evolving tradition. Its experience, teachings, and practices are not to be narrowed to the Gospels' accounts—they develop through a continuous revelation informed by the immanent Christ and the Fire of Life, the Spirit. Christ said: "All this I have spoken while still with you. But the Advocate, the Holy Spirit, whom the Father will send in my name, will teach you all things" (John 14:25–26).[35]

Through the indwelling Spirit, humanity becomes progressively aware of its genesis, as mediated by the Christ: the Logos, the Word. It is the importance of the Word in Christianity that should make the Christian an explorer of the effects of language—spoken and written[36]—in perception and life. After Christ's departure from the physical plane, he and the Father sent the Fire of Life to speak through us; hence, Christian testimony and teaching continues through the *living word*, which is the fruit of the Living Fire. Indeed, the Fire of Life resides with the Eternal Christ, the Logos, and so it is the Life of the Word (the very Word?). Jesus told his disciples not to worry about what they would say to defend themselves in times of persecution and trial—the Spirit would speak on those occasions.[37] Yet, not all times are of tribulation. If so, the preoccupation of the Christian becomes not what to say but rather *how we are to use words* so that we may experience the Light of Christ and contribute to the Divine Life we are to live. Christ said: "You will receive power when the Holy Spirit [the Fire of Life] comes on you; and you will be my witnesses in Jerusalem, and in all Judea and Samaria, and to the ends of the earth" (Acts 1:8).[38] Thus, we must understand how to *listen* to the Spirit so as to speak Life, Truth, and freedom.

---

35. In this line of thought, Symeon states: "But what is the key of knowledge other than the grace of the Holy Spirit given through faith? In very truth it produces knowledge and understanding through illumination and opens our closed and veiled mind (*cf. Lk.* 24:45) through many parables and symbols, as I have told you, as well as by clear proofs" (Symeon the New Theologian, *Discourses*, 341). See 1 Cor 2:6–16 on "God's wisdom" (2:7), revelation by the Spirit (2:10–15), and having "the mind of Christ" (2:16).

36. Written language is to be explored beyond its functional use—it plays a major role in bearing witness to Christ, but also in the development of Christian understanding and even Christian experience. Certainly, written language can be much more than transcribed speech; for example, it can be seen as the language of interiority—not always meant to be read out loud but engaged, inwardly, in contemplative silence, and so in close proximity with the Father, the Source.

37. Matt 10:19; Mark 13:11; Luke 12:11.

38. See Acts 1:3–8.

Truth

A Christian aware of the immanent Christ does not say, "Where is Christ?" "Where is God?" Such a Christian has realized that Christ's words "I will not leave you as orphans" and "I will come to you" were true; that Christ, indeed, *remained*. Christians shall pursue a living understanding of Christ's teaching, exploring ever-new avenues through the Spirit—the Fire of Life.[39] For, Christianity has no end, but lives eternally—in *us*.

---

39. The coming of the Fire of Life is not a one-time event. As in Acts 4:31, there is a repeated coming of the Holy Spirit since the beginning of Christianity. That is, there are *"recurring pentecostal outpourings"* that give "both boldness and confidence to the Church" (Gillquist, *Orthodox Study Bible*, 281; emphasis added, boldface removed). Both the reception of the Spirit and prophesy include men and women: "Your sons and your daughters shall prophesy . . . . And on My menservants and on My maidservants I will pour out My Spirit in those days; And they shall prophesy" (Acts 2:17–18 NKJV).

Bibliography

Aguilar, Mario I. *The Way of the Hermit: Interfaith Encounters in Silence and Prayer.* London: Jessica Kingsley, 2017. Kindle.
Augustine. *Confessions.* Translated by R. S. Pine-Coffin. London: Penguin, 1961.
———. *On the Trinity: Books 8–15.* Cambridge Texts in the History of Philosophy. Edited by Gareth B. Matthews. Translated by Stephen McKenna. New York: Cambridge University Press, 2002.
———. *St. Augustine's City of God and Christian Doctrine.* Nicene and Post-Nicene Fathers First Series 2. Edited by Philip Schaff. Grand Rapids: CCEL, 1890. https://www.ccel.org/ccel/schaff/npnf102.html.
Aurobindo, Sri. *Letters on Yoga.* The Complete Works of Sri Aurobindo 28. Vol. 1. Pondicherry: Sri Aurobindo Ashram, 2012. https://www.sriaurobindoashram.org/sriaurobindo/writings.php.
———. *Letters on Yoga.* The Complete Works of Sri Aurobindo 29. Vol. 2. Pondicherry: Sri Aurobindo Ashram, 2013. https://www.sriaurobindoashram.org/sriaurobindo/writings.php.
———. *The Life Divine.* The Complete Works of Sri Aurobindo 21–22. Pondicherry: Sri Aurobindo Ashram, 2005. https://www.sriaurobindoashram.org/sriaurobindo/writings.php.
Clooney, Francis X. *Learning Interreligiously: In the Text, in the World.* Minneapolis: Fortress, 2018.
Davila, James R. *Hekhalot Literature in Translation: Major Texts of Merkavah Mysticism.* Supplements to the Journal of Jewish Thought and Philosophy 20. Leiden: Brill, 2013.
Dionysius the Areopagite. *Pseudo-Dionysius: The Complete Works.* The Classics of Western Spirituality. Translated by Colm Luibheid and Paul Rorem. Mahwah, NJ: Paulist, 1987.
du Boulay, Shirley. *The Cave of the Heart: The Life of Swami Abhishiktananda.* Maryknoll: Orbis, 2005.
Fassberg, Steven E. "Which Semitic Language Did Jesus and Other Contemporary Jews Speak?" *Catholic Biblical Quarterly* 74 (2012) 263–80.
Gillquist, Peter E., et al., eds.*The Orthodox Study Bible: New Testament and Psalms, New King James Version.* Nashville: Thomas Nelson, 1993.
Gómez Pascual, María Ángeles. *La piedra y el aire: Poemas.* Madrid: ADI, 2002.
Hauerwas, Stanley. *Hannah's Child: A Theologian's Memoir.* Grand Rapids: Eerdmans, 2010. Kindle.

Bibliography

Huxley, Aldous. *The Divine Within: Selected Writings on Enlightenment*. New York: Harper Collins, 2013. Kindle.

Juan de la Cruz. *Obras completas*. Edited by José Vicente Rodríguez. Madrid: Editorial de Espiritualidad, 2009.

Levinas, Emmanuel. *Emmauel Levinas: Basic Philosophical Writings*. Edited by Adriaan T. Peperzak et al. Bloomington: Indiana University Press, 1996.

Miles-Yepez, Netanel, ed. *The Common Heart: An Experience of Interreligious Dialogue*. New York: Lantern, 2006. Kindle.

Mounce, William D., and Robert H. Mounce, eds. *The Zondervan Greek and English Interlinear New Testament (NASB/NIV)*. Grand Rapids: Zondervan Academic, 2008.

Müller, F. Max. *Natural Religion: The Gifford Lectures Delivered before the University of Glasgow in 1888*. New York: Longmans, Green & Co., 1889.

Palamas, Gregory. *The Triads*. The Classics of Western Spirituality. Edited by John Meyendorff. Translated by Nicholas Gendle. Mahwah, NJ: Paulist, 1983.

Panikkar, Raimon. *Christophany: The Fullness of Man*. Maryknoll: Orbis, 2004.

———. *The Intrareligious Dialogue*. New York: Paulist, 1999.

———. *The Rhythm of Being: The Gifford Lectures*. Maryknoll: Orbis, 2010.

———. *The Water of the Drop: Fragments from Panikkar's Diaries*. Edited by Milena Carrara Pavan. Delhi: ISPCK, 2018.

Panikkar, Raimundo. *The Trinity and the Religious Experience of Man*. Maryknoll: Orbis, 1973.

Pesce, Mauro. *De Jesús al cristianismo*. Translated by José Francisco Domínguez García. Madrid: San Pablo, 2017.

Portilla, Isaac. *The Possibilities of Spiritual Experience: An Autobiographical and Philosophical Exploration*. Madrid: Editorial Mirlo, 2017.

———. *El yoga del perdón: El perdón como estado del ser y otras exploraciones existenciales*. Enseñanzas y exploraciones existenciales 1. Edited by Juan Yusta. Madrid: Editorial Mirlo, 2020.

Rohr, Richard, and Mike Morrell. *The Divine Dance: The Trinity and Your Transformation*. London: SPCK, 2016.

Steindl-Rast, David. *i am through you so i: Reflections at Age 90*. Translated by Peter Dahm Robertson. New York: Paulist, 2017.

Symeon the New Theologian. *Divine Eros: Hymns of St. Symeon the New Theologian*. Translated by Daniel K. Griggs. New York: St. Vladimir's Seminary, 2010. Kindle.

———. *Symeon the New Theologian: The Discourses*. The Classics of Western Spirituality. Translated by C. J. de Catanzaro. Mahwah, NJ: Paulist, 1980.

Teresa de Jesús. *Castillo interior o las moradas*. Edited by José Vicente Rodríguez. Madrid: Editorial de Espiritualidad, 2006.

Wright, N. T. "Hope Deferred? Against the Dogma of Delay." *Early Christianity* 9 (2018) 37–82.

———. *Jesus and the Victory of God*. Christian Origins and the Question of God 2. London: SPCK, 1996.

www.ingramcontent.com/pod-product-compliance
Lightning Source LLC
Chambersburg PA
CBHW072152160426
43197CB00012B/2348